With the
LNER
in the Twenties

With the

LNER
in the Twenties

Humphrey Household

ALAN SUTTON
1985

Alan Sutton Publishing Limited
30 Brunswick Road
Gloucester GL1 1JJ

First Published 1985

British Library Cataloguing in Publication Data

Household, Humphrey
   With the LNER in the twenties.
   1. London and North Eastern Railway—History
   I. Title
   385′.0941   HE3020.L64

   ISBN 0-86299-226-5

Typesetting and origination by
Alan Sutton Publishing Limited
Printed in Great Britain
by Redwood Burn Limited,
Trowbridge

CONTENTS

With the LNER in the Twenties

INTRODUCTION

Looking back from my third quarter century to my first, it has been borne in on me that I emerged into what might be called 'an atmosphere of steam'. Steam-rollers grunted and growled outside the house from time to time, steam traction engines pulling wagons were met on country roads, perhaps halted at a bridge while replenishing tanks from a stream, steamers driven by paddlewheels whose engines could be watched at work ferried one across river or estuary, and above all there were the railway locomotives. Boys of my generation grew up while the popular cult of the steam railway was at its height, and most of us succumbed to its appeal to a greater or lesser extent. This it was that led me into the service of the London & North Eastern Railway.

I took many photographs, and it is these, and my experiences during four-and-a-half years of LNER training, which have prompted the production of this book. That company's North Eastern area figures largely, because those years were spent entirely in that region. This is no bad thing, because the old North Eastern Railway, although one of the four largest pre-grouping companies, received rather less attention in print and picture than many less important ones. Principally, this arose from its geographical position: it did not directly serve London. But I think there was also another reason: that it was primarily concerned with the movement of freight and mineral traffic and had not the glamorous expresses of the railways serving the south, south-west, midlands and north-west. Even the splendid Anglo-Scottish trains of the East Coast route were more often photographed on the Great Northern than the North Eastern.

It was an enterprising company in many ways, particularly in its attitude to electrification. Its steam locomotives were efficient and outstandingly handsome, but traditional, in that they did not lead to development of the locomotive in the way that those of the Great Western did, and the LNER under Sir Nigel Gresley. Its coaches, though reasonably comfortable, were not notable, apart from those it built for the East Coast Joint Stock which were, in fact, of Great Northern design. Its stations, however, were exceptionally good, and large ones among the finest in the land, and even most of the smaller ones designed by architects of taste.

Not until recent years have the railways of the north-east received the attention they deserve – at the hands of Ken Hoole who has devoted much time to the collection and publication of old photographs and detailed description of the various routes. He has used quite a number of mine taken in the 'twenties, but although some others have appeared in magazines, mostly nearly sixty years ago, there are many which have not previously been published.

I am grateful to the Editor of Country Life for permission to make use of an article of mine which appeared in his pages a few years ago recounting my experiences on wayside stations, and similarly to the National Motor Museum at Beaulieu in whose *Veteran & Vintage Magazine* my account of the early road services between Newcastle and London was printed. A chance enquiry from Neil Sinclair of Tyne & Wear County Council's Museums led to most valuable help: his fully illustrated booklet about the River Wear refreshed my memory of the area in which lay two of the wayside stations where I worked, and he enabled me to get in touch with Colin Alexander of Tynemouth who kindly provided me with a photograph of Tynemouth goods station where I began my LNER service. The City Archivist of Kingston-upon-Hull was very helpful in answering enquiries about the docks and in finding for me a plan of them, which Lloyd's of London Press Ltd have kindly given me permission to reproduce. I am also grateful to Richard Graham who has been researching the history of railway companies' staff magazines; and to the *Newcastle Chronicle & Journal*, the North York Moors Historical Railway Trust, the Science Museum, and the National Railway Museum, for permission to use photographs. Last, but by no means least, the Railway Room in Ashford Public Library of Kent County Council has been a very valuable source of information; and my thanks are due to the staff at the Guildhall Camera Centre, Folkestone, for the care and trouble they have taken in copying old photographs and printing my own, often no easy task.

Humphrey Household
Folkestone,
June 1985

CHAPTER ONE

THE APPEAL OF THE RAILWAY

The railways reached their zenith in popular esteem during the last decade of the nineteenth century. By then, anyone bound for distant places on business or pleasure had to travel by train: there was no other way; stage coaches had long since vanished from routes served by rail; the motor vehicle was in its infancy. Public interest in railway matters, especially steam locomotives, was therefore widespread. The names by which the railway companies were known (and all but one continued to be known until the end of 1922) had been familiar for thirty-five to sixty years. Most of those names had a strong territorial association, stimulating regional loyalty and, frequently, ardent partisanship.

Journals for investors and engineers had long been in circulation, but in the late 1890s there appeared magazines appealing to popular interest, lavishly illustrated, including colour plates of engines and trains: *Moore's Monthly Magazine* was published in January 1896 and became *The Locomotive Magazine* a year later with a long run ahead; *The Railway Magazine* began its even longer run in 1897. In the book trade also, technical publications were supplemented by popular ones. Ward Lock's *Wonder Book of Railways*, first published about 1906, catered for the very young. There were 'Boys' Books' of locomotives and railways. For readers of all ages there were more sophisticated studies, lavishly illustrated, such as *Our Home Railways* by W.J. Gordon, 1910, and *Railway Wonders of the World* by F.A. Talbot, 1913.

The picture postcard had spread from the Continent to Britain by about 1894, and it was not long before illustrations of locomotives and trains were added to scenic views, several of the railway companies themselves marketing them, the Great Northern as early as 1897: Midland, Great Western, Great Eastern, Lancashire & Yorkshire, Caledonian, South Eastern & Chatham, Furness, were others. Above all, there was the London & North Western, whose informative sets were so eagerly collected that one of their 1913 cards asserted: 'Over 10 million sold'. Many publishers, particularly Valentine of Dundee and W.H. Smith & Son, issued cards of engines, trains, bridges and innumerable stations. In colour, there were Raphael Tuck's Oilette Series of Famous Expresses, British and Foreign, and the Locomotive Publishing Company's cards painted from photographs with the signature 'F. Moore' guaranteeing accuracy.

Modelling had begun with examples intended to convince directors of the merits of a new design, notably the model of the *Royal George* made by Timothy Hackworth in 1827 for the Stockton & Darlington directors. Engineers also built models for their own private pleasure: long in my possession, and now in the North Western Museum of Science & Industry, is one made about 1850, bearing an inscribed brass plate, 'Michael Noton, Engineer, Salford', my maternal great-great-uncle. In a railway age, however, model trains had their maximum appeal as a child's toy. Primitive floor trains, pushed by hand, were available commercially as early as 1835. Small steam locomotives were marketed in the 'sixties, but as they were expensive and curves round which they could run safely took up a lot of space, they were toys for the well-to-do living in spacious houses; more-

Original model of the *Royal George* made by Timothy Hackworth, locomotive engineer of the Stockton & Darlington Railway, for approval by the directors. The engine was built in 1827 and worked successfully until 1842. (*Photograph: Trustees of the Science Museum.*)

Model made by Michael Noton, Engineer, Salford, about 1850. Eighteen inches long, it resembles Robert Stephenson's *Planet* type of 1830–35. It has a boiler lagged with mahogany, brass motion, copper firebox with grate for solid fuel, and its axles are set to run on a circular track.

over, the risk of fire made it unsafe to let a child use one unless supervised.

Cheaper to manufacture, and safer in small hands, was the clockwork engine. German toy-makers developed these, one of the best known, Marklin Brothers, popularising the model railway by standardising gauges, making tinplate rails and points in lengths and of curvature which could easily be assembled in geometric form, and by adding to locomotives and rolling stock accessories such as stations, signal boxes and signals, all of which appeared in their catalogues in the 1890s. At first limited to the larger gauges 3, 2 and 1, these soon became available in the cheaper gauge 0. Bing Brothers, the largest toy makers in the world, followed Marklin's lead by 1898.

The appearance of commercially produced locomotives and rolling stock was, however, crude, until W.J. Bassett-Lowke of Northampton collaborated with Bing in 1900 to make scale models of British locomotives. Another German firm, Carette, made tinplate coaches and wagons to Bassett-Lowke's requirements. Between the three of them, types in use on all the leading British railways became available in the early 1900s at prices well within the range of middle class pockets: in 1909, for example, a gauge 0 clockwork Great Northern Atlantic for £1 10*s*. 6*d*., coaches for 5*s*. 6*d*., wagons for as little as 1*s*. 10*d*. Well before the 1914–18 war put a stop to further manufacture, a boy was therefore able to build up a convincing model railway as gifts and pocket-money permitted.

11

Hearing the talk of his elders comparing the performance of new locomotives and the speed, comfort and cuisine offered by rival railway routes, and himself having the opportunity to collect coloured plates, picture postcards, models and suitable books, a boy of the early 1900s grew up imbued with the romance of steam and the rail, and a common answer from the immature to the question, 'What will you do when you are grown up?' was 'I want to be an engine driver'.

Of course some were infected more than others. My elder brother, always interested, though never an addict like myself, was given for his sixth birthday in 1906 a complete railway outfit, which, my father recorded, gave him great pleasure. My greater interest showed when I was only nineteen months old and insisted, while we were on holiday, on being taken 'to the station before breakfast to see the train come in', and that was the inglorious Great Western local from Taunton to Minehead! Before I was three, I was asking 'how steam made an engine work'. On walks with a devoted and understanding Nanny, I would become a locomotive, puffing valiantly, arms going to and fro as pistons, stopping at intervals because an invisible signal was against me.

I was given my own clockwork engine at the age of six, and as my brother's interests widened, the model railway became my inheritance, but I could only add to it slowly because it was gauge 1 and its equipment that much more expensive, especially the scale models for which I yearned – I was given a magnificent coach in London & South Western livery with a roof hinged to reveal an interior fitted with (tinplate) cushioned seats and luggage racks, but I never approved of its gargantuan proportions. Midland styling was my preference, so I acquired two clerestory coaches, but as dining car and postal van were made only to LNWR designs, my passenger train had to include stock of two unfriendly rivals. The old tinplate track was replaced by a type with wooden sleepers and, better still, some Lowko rails and pointwork in chairs on sleepers more closely spaced. But Bassett-Lowke engines were by then unobtainable, so I had to wait for the first model marketed after the end of the war, an LNWR 4-4-2 Precursor tank.

All was later sold to finance the expensive hobby of photography, in which railway subjects gradually acquired an ascendency. Brought up in Cheltenham as I was, journeys were almost all made over the Great Western, the Midland, or the Midland & South Western Junction, with only occasional forays on the LNWR and LSWR. But visits to Manchester provided the opportunity to see Great Central locomotives there and at Stockport Teviot Dale, where one of my early photographs was taken. My first journey over that company's tracks was made in the late autumn of 1923, to Rugby by the Swansea–Newcastle express, taken over at Banbury by one of the graceful Great Central Atlantics. Little did I think that in two years' time I should be aboard that same train, making for the north-east and railway service.

The author's model railway in 1921: Bassett-Lowke LNWR Precursor tank locomotive, 12-wheeled dining car, postal van, Midland clerestory coach, and assorted goods wagons. Walls decorated with railway postcards, coloured plates, and a shipping poster!

Great Central 0-6-0 with a goods train running through Stockport Teviot Dale station, Cheshire Lines Committee, 27 April 1922.

For of course, railway employment had long been my goal. Influenced, perhaps, by stories of great-great-uncle Michael's prowess as an engineer, my imagination had been stirred by the glamour of locomotive design, so my final year at school was concentrated upon a narrow curriculum aimed at a Higher Certificate which would be the gateway to a course in engineering. However, I was waylaid by the rational and irrational* denizens lurking in the dark and gloomy forest of higher mathematics, so engineering was not for me. Nevertheless, there was the alternative of the traffic and administrative side of railway operation. It was not easy to gain entry, and a first attempt failed.

Meantime there were visits to friends in Cambridge, the first in April 1924 from Devon via Waterloo and King's Cross, carefully arranged so that I should be able to spend about two hours at the Great Northern terminus. After all, Gresley's Pacifics were still new and splendid, and I hoped to photograph one. I was not disappointed: 1475 was on the turntable and presently backed down to the 4 p.m. for York and Newcastle-upon-Tyne. Much else was to be seen. A two-cylinder 'Ragtime' 2-6-0, a well-proportioned Great Northern design of 1912 (hence the nickname), departed in a flurry of steam from open drain-cocks. Gresley 0-6-2 tanks pounded noisily up the steep gradient from the Metropolitan line to the suburban platform, and the Harrogate Pullman drew in, headed by *Lord Stuart of Wortley*, one of Robinson's four-cylinder 4-6-0 engines transferred from the Great Central.

A longer visit to Cambridge the following October was a golden opportunity for fresh railway photography. I found an ideal stance beside the Trumpington level crossing (later bridged), just south of the City – ideal within limitations, that is, for it was a position suiting southbound trains only, those from the London direction coming out of the sun through a belt of trees. At that date, pre-grouping liveries were still to be seen everywhere, though fading, but the splendid Great Eastern Royal Blue had long since succumbed to wartime battleship grey, and 4-6-0 No 1550 on a freight train was eclipsed by her sister 8533 resplendent in LNER apple green. It was an interesting site, as a relief line from Cambridge converged with the main just short of the level crossing. Three of my photographs of passenger trains show a freight train standing in the loop, all of which I took as they drew out once the line ahead was clear. One, of a King's Cross train, also shows a platelaying gang at work, extending the Great Eastern's stub catch-points to give greater clearance in case of overrunning. Close by was the LNWR line to Bletchley and Oxford, over which that more prosperous company had taken the road by a bridge.

* Lest I should be suspected of hyperbole, I quote the *Concise Oxford Dictionary*: 'Surd, Mathematics, Irrational (number, especially root of integer).'

14

King's Cross, 26 April 1924. Gresley Pacific No 1475, not then bearing a name, on the 4 p.m. to York and Newcastle.

King's Cross. Great Northern 2-cylinder 2-6-0 No 1679 setting off. The class, designed by H.N. Gresley, first appeared in 1912, hence the nickname 'Ragtime'.

The Harrogate Pullman, 9.30 a.m. from Newcastle, arriving at King's Cross behind Great Central 4-cylinder 4-6-0 No. 6168 *Lord Stuart of Wortley*.

As future railway employment then seemed unlikely, I took what was on offer and became a trainee with a manufacturing company in East London. It offered good prospects, but no escape from the tedium of office routine. However, I acquired a temperamental motor-bicycle with whose reluctant co-operation I spent Saturday afternoons and Sundays visiting lineside sites on the South Eastern & Chatham, Brighton, Great Eastern, Tilbury, District, Metropolitan & Great Central Joint Line, in search of photographs. I had no permits, so I had to choose my sites with care, but with the help of Ordnance Survey maps it was not difficult to find a level crossing, or a public footpath across the tracks in the countryside, or an overline bridge where I could slip inconspicuously down the cutting-side. My chosen site on the Brighton line gave me a shock, for having climbed down into a deep cutting, I found myself in full view of a signal box. There was nothing for it but to make my presence known. I did so with some anxiety, but I need not have worried, for I was immediately invited up and given detailed information of each train as it approached. This not only laid the foundations of a friendship which long persisted, but also established a confidence, which never proved to be misplaced, that an appeal to a signalman would meet, not with a rebuff, but a welcome. The most difficult viewpoint to reach was obviously one alongside the busy electrified lines of the District Railway, but here my mother made a lucky strike, talking a senior official at Acton Town into taking me under his wing and giving me an evening and a morning of rare privilege.

16

Cambridge. Up express, 7.42 a.m. ex Yarmouth, 8.47 a.m. ex Norwich, to Liverpool Street (this service via Cambridge was later discontinued). Great Eastern 1500 class locomotive No 8533, one of the series built 1912–17, in LNER livery. A freight train can be seen waiting on the relief line. 18 October 1924.

Up goods drawing out of the relief line to follow the express, drawn by No 1550, one of twenty of the 1500 class built by William Beardmore & Co., Glasgow, in 1920–21, in faded GE livery. 18 October 1924.

17

Up restaurant car express from Norwich with coaches from Yarmouth and Hunstanton. 4-6-0 No 1520. 18 October 1924.

Cambridge to Haverhill and Colchester train. GE 4-4-0 No 7748. 18 October 1924.

Cambridge–King's Cross train hauled by Great Northern Atlantic No 1441, one of H.A. Ivatt's 1902 design. Freight train waiting on the relief line, and permanent way gang at work on the catch points. 20 October 1924.

Up goods leaving the relief line. GE 0-6-0 No 8274 was one of A.J. Hill's class built 1920–22 with the same boiler as the 1500 class, the largest and most powerful 0-6-0s in Britain, except for the much later Southern Railway Q1 class. 20 October 1924.

4-4-0 No 4388, Ivatt's first design after appointment to the GN in 1896, on Cambridge–King's Cross train. 24 October 1924.

Cambridge–Haverhill train passing a train of cattle wagons standing on the relief line. GE 2-4-0 No 469 of James Holden's T26 mixed traffic class, of which a hundred were built 1891–1902. 24 October 1924.

Train composed entirely of GWR cattle wagons, probably returning empty to Fishguard. GE 0-6-0 No 886, one of 115 class Y14 built to James Holden's design 1886–90, with dome set unusually far forward. 24 October 1924.

When six months had passed, the gloom of East London was dispelled by the rosy, and wholly unexpected, prospect of railway service after all. So the motor-bike, camera and I departed for Cheltenham. From there I took more photographs of Gloucestershire railways, ranging further afield than in my schooldays; and when my father and I went off for a fortnight's holiday in Wales in August 1925, there were delightful narrow gauge railways to see. I managed to visit a considerable number of those within reach, more indeed than my father could stomach, in spite of his sympathetic understanding and their uniformly lovely setting. I determined to write up these, bombarding the managements with questionnaires to which they replied encouragingly. The Glyn Valley Tramway was the first I covered, and I was delighted when the handwritten article, illustrated by my own photographs, was accepted by the editor of *The Railway Magazine*, and later when the postman delivered a cheque, for thirty shillings! It proved to be the first of quite a series. The next was the Talyllyn, and that likewise was accepted at once, but when it appeared I found that it was an ill-kneaded dough made by mixing my article with one sent in by another contributor. I wrote angrily to the editor, J.F. Gairns, claiming that had a proof been sent to either author, the finished product would have had a smoother texture. It was twenty-four years before I sent anything else to *The Railway Magazine*, and my subsequent articles on narrow gauge and light railways appeared in *The Locomotive Railway Carriage and Wagon Review*, with whose proprietors, A.R. and A.M. Bell, there developed a friendly understanding that any reasonable contribution I submitted was likely to be accepted – a happy state indeed.

21

Brentwood, 6 June 1925. These four trains were photographed between 5.30 and 6 p.m.
2.24 p.m. Yarmouth–Liverpool Street express. GE 4-6-0 No 8523.

Southend–Liverpool Street train. The first three coaches are six-wheeled, and make up a
strange assortment for a locomotive specially maintained for working Royal Trains: No 8783,
one of the Super-Clauds, the last batch of the splendid Claud Hamilton class as improved by
A.J. Hill in 1923.

5.18 p.m. Liverpool Street to Cromer and Sheringham dining car express. GE 4-6-0 No 8557, another of those built by Beardmore.

Up Chelmsford suburban train, a close-coupled set of bogie coaches of the type reconstructed by A.J. Hill from 1915 onwards by mounting bodies of old four-wheelers in pairs on new frames. 0-6-0 No 7640.

Metropolitan & Great Central Joint Line, 22 August 1925. The first four photographs were taken near Great Missenden, the last two at Harrow-on-the-Hill. Up express hauled by GC Improved Director class 4-4-0 No 5505 *Ypres*, built at Gorton Works 1922.

Metropolitan Aylesbury train, including one of the company's two Pullman cars used from 1910 to 1939. The 4-4-4 tank engine is No 106 of class H, one of eight designed by Charles Jones and built by Kerr Stuart in 1920–21.

Metropolitan Baker Street train hauled by 0-6-4 No 95 *Robert H. Selbie* of class G, one of four powerful tank locomotives designed by Charles Jones and built by the Yorkshire Engine Co., in 1915.

Metropolitan down goods train behind 2-6-4 No 114 class K, one of six erected by Armstrong Whitworth in 1925 from parts made at Woolwich Arsenal to Maunsell's SE&CR 2-6-0 design to provide employment after the end of the 1914–18 war. Sold off cheap by the Disposals Board, these parts needed only assembly and the addition of newly made side tanks, bunkers, cabs and rear bogies.

Marylebone–Manchester express with through coach to Halifax. Improved Director 4-4-0 No 5511 *Marne* (built 1922) piloting Robinson Atlantic.

Metropolitan seven-car train. This was the earliest type of multiple-unit train used on the electrified lines north of Baker Street, introduced in 1906 after modification of outer suburban bogie compartment steam stock, which had been built by the Ashbury Carriage & Wagon Co. from 1898 onwards.

CHAPTER TWO

THE LNER TAKES SHAPE

The London & North Eastern Railway was born on 1 January 1923, one of the four large companies formed as the outcome of the Railways Act of 1921, by which Parliament decreed that 120 independent railway companies should be merged into groups. The Great Western alone preserved its identity, and, after swallowing the Cambrian and a number of railways serving the mining valleys and ports of South Wales, remained largely unchanged.

The London Midland & Scottish, the biggest of the four, was an unwieldy hotchpotch of disparate elements, including two of the four largest pre-grouping companies, the London & North Western and the Midland, whose previous animosity resolved into a bitter struggle for paramount influence, until, in 1926, a strong hand was brought in from industry to weld the parts into a whole. Adopting the American method of organisation, Sir Josiah Stamp (later Lord Stamp) took the title of President, with a team of Vice-Presidents, each heading a department. Even so, in locomotive matters sparring between Crewe and Derby continued over questions great and small (Crewe, for example, defiantly continuing to paint its locomotives black although the official livery for passenger engines was Midland red) until in 1932 W.A. Stanier came from Swindon as Chief Mechanical Engineer. Overriding petty jealousies, Stanier quickly took up the long-overdue task of providing the LMS with a stud of powerful modern locomotives, based, with modifications, on the well-established GWR tradition.

The Southern spent an uncertain year under the joint control of the three general managers of its principal constituents, until two of the three retired, leaving Sir Herbert Walker of the London & South Western in command; he had, after all, been Chairman of the Railway Executive Committee which had managed the railway system as a whole for the government during the first world war. A very great railwayman with progressive ideas,

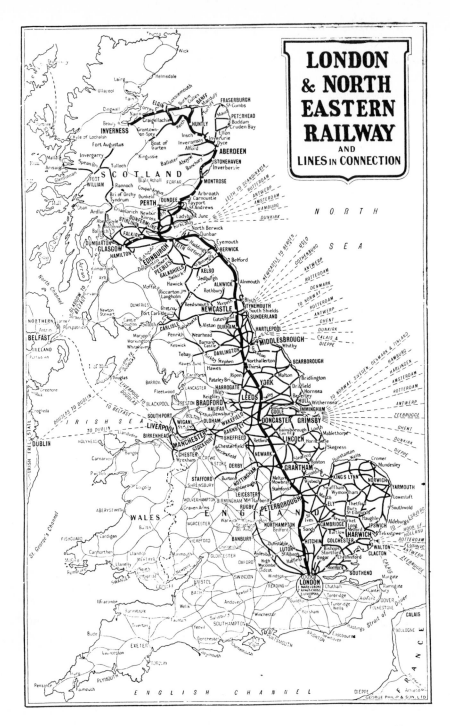

Map of the London & North Eastern Railway, from the LNER Timetable pre-1933.
(*Photostat supplied by the National Railway Museum.*)

particularly with regard to electrification, he restored the three railways, all severely strained by five years of intensive wartime service to the Channel Ports, and in thirteen years thereafter he made the Southern a great railway.

The London & North Eastern was spared internal bickering between powerful rivals. It comprised seven previously independent railways, three of which, the Great Northern, North Eastern and North British, had long co-operated in maintaining the services by the East Coast route from King's Cross to Scotland. Moreover, only a dozen years earlier, in 1909, the Great Northern, Great Eastern and Great Central had very sensibly proposed unification under a joint managing committee, but the Bill to give it effect had been rejected by a Parliament still intent upon encouraging maximum competition, although the three only competed to a limited extent. In addition to the five already named, there were the Great North of Scotland which extended the East Coast route northwards from Aberdeen, and the Hull & Barnsley, a wholly unnecessary railway promoted by citizens of Kingston-upon-Hull who considered the North Eastern's monopoly of the area put them at a disadvantage.

The North Eastern Railway was the largest, and by far the strongest constituent of the group, because of the volume of freight and mineral traffic generated in its industrial area and the steady west–east flow of coal from

North Eastern mineral train at Hett, near Ferryhill, County Durham, drawn by class S3 3-cylinder 4-6-0 No 2374. All NER mineral traffic was carried in the company's own wagons, not in private owner wagons as in most parts of Britain. Many of them, carrying 20 tons, had tall tapering sides and bottom doors for discharge at iron and steel works, and at retail coal depots at local stations where the stationmaster was also coal agent. The greater capacity of these wagons made for more economical transport than in 10 or 12 ton private owner wagons. 29 May 1926.

mines to east coast ports for shipment. The company was proud of its lineage, stemming from the beginning of the railway age when the opening of the Stockton & Darlington in 1825 created the image of the public, as distinct from the private, railway operated by steam locomotives. Not unnaturally, North Eastern men saw their old company as the senior partner in the new, but they did not have it all their own way, though many of their men filled leading positions. That outstanding railwayman, Sir Sam Fay, the enterprising General Manager of the Great Central since 1902, might have been chosen to head the LNER, but he was sixty-six at the end of 1922. Another was the able General Manager of the Great Eastern, Sir Henry Thornton, an American; but frustrated in an ambitious alternative scheme of his own devising, he accepted an invitation to become President of the Canadian National Railways, and quitted the Great Eastern in November 1922 to cross the Atlantic once again.

The North Eastern's own General Manager, Sir Alexander Kaye Butterworth, an able lawyer who played a leading part in the complicated financial arrangements of the merger, was another well qualified to take charge, but as he would then be sixty-eight his tenure could not last long, whereas it was obvious that the chief officer of the new LNER ought to be one able to remain in office for some time. His deputy, then aged forty-eight clearly was such a one, so it was agreed that Butterworth should resign at the end of 1921, giving R.L. Wedgwood a year as head of his old company before assuming command of the new. Great-great-grandson of Josiah,

North Eastern Railway freight train at Hett, a long train of typically mixed stock: open wagons, high-sided mineral wagons, and covered vans. Class P3 0-6-0 No 2392. 29 May 1926.

founder of the world famous pottery firm, Ralph Wedgwood had been educated at Clifton College and Trinity College, Cambridge. A man of great ability, he had already shown an exceptional capacity for hard work and organisation, for during the 1914–18 war he had held simultaneously the posts of chief goods manager and passenger manager, and had added that of deputy general manager in 1919. The choice could not have been better: he proved to be an outstanding railway manager, and guided the new company for more than sixteen years until he retired in March 1939.

The Chairman was William Whitelaw, a Scot with long experience of railway management. For twenty years he had been chairman, first of the Highland, later of the North British, neither of them prosperous, so that he had had to watch expenditure closely, something he continued to do, though not oppressively, on the LNER for sixteen years. Fortunate it is when the chairman of the Board and the chief officer work together for a long period as harmoniously as Whitelaw and Wedgwood did. Other directors also devoted much time to the company's affairs, for a seat on the Board was no sinecure: they sat on the various departmental committees, and their outside interests were valuable, not only commercially, but also by bringing knowledge of the outer business world into what tended to be a close community of railwaymen.

The charismatic post of Chief Mechanical Engineer, designer of the locomotives which monopolised the public eye, is said to have been offered to J.G. Robinson, who since 1900 had designed for the Great Central a stud of handsome and successful engines; but he was sixty-six and felt it wise to decline. Another contender was Sir Vincent Raven, who had been Chief Mechanical Engineer of the North Eastern for twelve years. Besides producing capable steam locomotives, Raven held advanced views on main line electrification; but he also was well over sixty. The obvious choice, then, was H.N. Gresley, forty-six years old. Scion of a Derbyshire county family and grandson of the holder of an original baronetcy, Gresley had been since 1911 Chief Mechanical Engineer of the Great Northern, for which he had built powerful engines of modern design. Again, the choice could not have been better, for Gresley had an enquiring and receptive mind, and learnt much from others, first from the Churchward-Collett régime at Swindon, and later from the great French engineer, André Chapelon, thereby putting himself in the forefront of British locomotive engineering and richly deserving the knighthood bestowed on him in 1936, one of the very few, probably indeed the only one, awarded for mechanical engineering and organisation, rather than for government service.

The system of management evolved by Wedgwood and the Board differed completely from that adopted by any other railway company in Britain. Eschewing alike the traditional organisation followed by the Great Western and the Southern, under a general manager and chief officers, and the departmental system under Vice-Presidents which Stamp had introduced

31

on the LMS, the LNER adopted regional divisions, each with its own general manager and departmental officers, with a limited number of all–line appointments, under Wedgwood as Chief General Manager at King's Cross. The Great Northern, Great Eastern and Great Central were combined in the Southern Area, the largest of the three, with headquarters at Liverpool Street. The North British and Great North of Scotland formed the Scottish Area with headquarters in Edinburgh. The North Eastern, which had absorbed the Hull & Barnsley nine months in advance of the grouping, became the North Eastern Area, managed from the old company's headquarters building in York.

The arrangement worked very well; susceptibilities were not ruffled; the transition was smooth. The three forming the Southern Area had, after all, been ready for union in 1909 and had co–operated closely thereafter. The proud North Eastern had provided the Chief General Manager, and was virtually autonomous with one of its own officers, Alex Wilson, as Area General Manager. The Southern Area had to be placed, by virtue of seniority, under S.A. Parnwell, although his experience was limited as he had followed Sir Henry Thornton at Liverpool Street only two months

Spey Viaduct, Garmouth, on the Moray Firth coast line of the Great North of Scotland Railway, was opened in 1886. As the Spey is notorious for destructive floods and alterations of its bed, the viaduct across the estuary was built with a bowstring girder 350 feet long, and three spans of 100 feet at each end. When this photograph was taken in June 1970, the rails had been removed and the fine structure no longer served any useful purpose.

before. The Scottish Area manager was James Calder, General Manager of the North British since 1918. The Great North of Scotland, far from finding itself ignored, saw George Davidson, its able and experienced General Manager for sixteen years, take charge of the NE Area in 1924, when Parnwell was persuaded to retire (with lavish compensation!) and Alex Wilson moved south to succeed him. Davidson's tenure was unfortunately short, however, as he died suddenly while on holiday in 1928.

The names of railway general managers were usually widely known, appearing on publicity material and catching the limelight in the Honours List, for most of those heading the leading companies were offered, and few declined, a knighthood, Ralph Wedgwood receiving his in 1924. The locomotive superintendents, or chief mechanical engineers, were also widely known because of general interest in their machines – it was, after all, their locomotives which maintained the services, and their coaches in which the passengers rode, more or less comfortably as might be the case. But however good those trains were, their smooth passage depended upon how well the civil engineers maintained the track and bridges. Great Northern track was laid and maintained to a standard of excellence far surpassing that of the other LNER constituents, even of all other railways except the London & North Western; the superiority was obvious to passengers travelling by the East Coast route from King's Cross. Yet the LNER did not appoint a chief civil engineer until near the end of its existence; C.J. Brown, Chief Engineer of the Great Northern, took charge also of the Great Central in 1923 and of the whole Southern Area in 1925, when John Miller of the Great Eastern became civil engineer of the NE Area. In a dozen years, Miller achieved much needed improvement of NE track, and, a nice touch, saw to the tidying up of unsightly lineside patches by planting those grass plots within neat concrete verges which became such a pleasing characteristic.

There were many other important officers. The Superintendent, or Superintendent of the Line, was head of the department which allocated coaching stock to particular services, allowing spares for replacement and strengthening crowded trains, organised wagon distribution, and planned the timetables. The Secretary had legal responsibilities which led to his name appearing on every railway-owned road vehicle, and also on the cast iron notice boards warning against trespass – some of these indestructible relics recording the name of an officer long departed! The LNER appointed joint Secretaries, both in offices at Marylebone, one from the Great Eastern, the other from the North British with the essential knowledge of Scottish law. To deal with the more intricate cases, there was a Chief Legal Adviser, also at Marylebone, Sir Francis Dunnell, a lawyer of great ability and distinction who had formerly been secretary and solicitor to the North Eastern. And among the all-line officers, there was an Advertising Manager, W.M. Teasdale from the North Eastern, who was responsible for some brilliant publicity and commissioning artistic posters.

The chief mechanical engineer had a very large department to organise, so that his chief draughtsman had much to do with the final appearance, and sometimes even the performance, of new locomotives. On the North Eastern, Wilson Worsdell's chief draughtsman, Walter M. Smith, had been entirely responsible for the design of two fine four-cylinder compound Atlantics in 1906, and developed a system of compounding widely adopted by the Midland and later the LMS. E.S. Tiddeman, the chief draughtsman at Stratford Works, is believed to have had a great deal more to do with the design of the Great Eastern 1500 class 4-6-0 engines than did his chief, Stephen Holden who resigned at the early age of forty-two not long after those very successful locomotives had appeared in 1912.

After the grouping of 1923, the locomotive policy of the four companies followed slightly different lines. The Great Western was able to continue the Churchward tradition unimpeded. On the LMS, although a few loco-motives of LNWR and Caledonian types were built, and many, including new designs, with Lancashire & Yorkshire characteristics, Midland types became standard until the advent of W.A. Stanier. On the Southern, R.E.L. Maunsell's Ashford team developed previous SE&CR practice, using Belpaire boilers, but he accepted the preference of Eastleigh's drawing office for round-topped fireboxes, and several of their LSWR designs were adopted as Southern Railway standards. On the LNER, Gresley's attitude towards existing designs was still more liberal. His own splendid Great Northern Pacifics and 2-6-0s were built in large numbers for widespread use on the system, but two of Robinson's Great Central types, and two Great Eastern classes, were augmented, and a new class of goods locomotive was designed at Darlington closely based on previous North Eastern practice. New 4-6-2 tank engines of Robinson's 1911 design appeared, not only on GC suburban services, but also around Newcastle and on Tees-side, and twenty-four of his Improved Director class, described by E.L. Ahrons in 1927 as 'amongst the most successful of the 4-4-0 type in the country' and 'representative of the best modern British practice', were built for service in Scotland.

The Great Eastern types also were not confined to their home beat. Ten more were added to the 1500 class in 1928; these remarkable locomotives, of which there were then eighty, were able to develop far greater power than their size suggested, and their modest adhesion weight of 43½ tons enabled a number displaced by Gresley's three-cylinder Sandringham class in 1928 to be sent north to work on the Great North of Scotland lines. At a later stage, many were reboilered by Gresley, but with the distinctive Great Eastern splashers cut away above the coupling rod and the neat copper-capped chimney replaced by a far less graceful design, they were no longer as handsome as they had been. Nevertheless, they proved very useful during the Second World War, when even the slight increase in total weight from 63 to 69¼ tons still gave them remarkable route availability, and they were

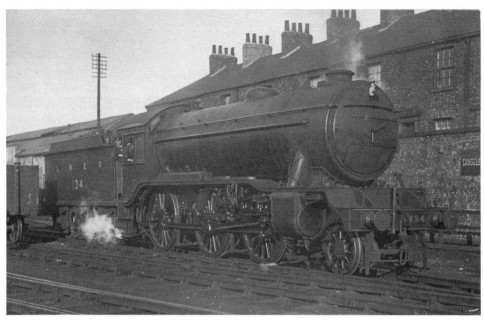

Gresley 3-cylinder 2-6-0 No 134, a Great Northern design of 1920 modified with shortened chimney and roomy cab of North Eastern type for general service over the LNER. At York, 23 July 1927.

Gresley Pacific No 2571 *Sunstar* at York, 7 May 1927.

Great Central Aylesbury suburban train near Great Missenden, drawn by 4-6-2 tank locomotive No 5007, one of those built for the LNER by Hawthorn Leslie & Co. in 1925 to Robinson's class 9N design of 1911. His suburban coaches, also a 1911 design, set a high standard of comfort. 22 August 1925.

One of J.G. Robinson's Improved Director class 4-4-0s built in 1924 with cut down boiler mountings for service in Scotland. No 6381 *Flora McIvor* leaving Waverley station for Glasgow on 11 June 1927. Her smokebox door was decorated with one of the steel stars characteristic of Scottish enginemen.

attached to ambulance trains which might be sent off at a moment's notice to a great variety of destinations.

A.J. Hill, the Works Manager at Stratford who succeeded Stephen Holden as locomotive, carriage and wagon superintendent in 1912, had considerably developed the Great Eastern tradition, designing locomotives with greatly increased power. The twenty-two 0-6-2 tank engines he had introduced to replace 0-6-0 and 2-4-2 tank engines on the Liverpool Street suburban services proved so efficient that the design was adopted as an LNER standard, and 112 more were added between 1925 and 1928, some of which were used on Great Northern suburban trains.

The Darlington contribution was two classes of 0-6-0 tender engines developed from the North Eastern class P3. Class J39, introduced in 1926, was intended for general goods working, but, with 5ft 2in driving wheels, was also useful for local passenger and excursion trains. It obviously proved its value, as others were built as late as 1941. Class J38 was similar, but with 4ft 8in wheels for mineral traffic in Scotland.

As they became due for repainting, passenger locomotives with driving wheels 6ft 6in or more in diameter appeared in Great Northern green; others, and all goods engines, were black. New coaching stock followed Great Northern and East Coast Joint Stock tradition, with wide Pullman gangways and the strong Buckeye couplers which reduced the risk of telescoping in accidents. Some were formed in complete new trains, such as that for the Great Eastern's Hook Continental in 1925. All coaches rapidly acquired the new livery, their teak bodies unpainted but highly varnished, Great Northern style, and a great improvement on the rather drab shades of crimson lake in vogue on the North Eastern, Great Eastern and North British; Great Central carriages had long appeared in varnished teak, as the Great Eastern's had done prior to 1919. The livery gave the passenger rolling stock a most attractive finish, completely different to that of the other three groups, until the adoption of steel side sheets made brown paint necessary in an unconvincing attempt to simulate varnished teak.

With freight rolling stock, little change was to be seen on any of the four groups, except that the four-wheeled wagons of many different types, the great majority without continuous brakes, acquired new initials. LMS fitted nicely, the middle letter on drop sides or sliding doors; but the other three opted for two letters only. GW and SR were obvious, but what of the third? Why, NE of course! It was neat; on a total of some 290,000 wagons, the painting of two initials instead of three was an obvious economy; nearly forty-four per cent of that total already bore those two initials; the remaining fifty-six per cent had in any case to be relettered when repair or repainting became necessary; and if it gave North Eastern men the feeling, never quite lost, that in reality their great company had absorbed the other six, what did it matter?

By 1927 the LNER had acquired a corporate identity, and in a message

Class J39 0-6-0, an LNER standard for general goods traffic designed at Darlington and introduced in 1926. No 1450 passing Alne on an up main line freight on 16 July 1927.

The new set of LNER coaches provided for the Harwich Continental service from Liverpool Street in April 1925, posed on Brentwood Bank with Great Eastern 4-6-0 No 8558. From a contemporary postcard.

published in the first issue of the all-line *London & North Eastern Railway Magazine* that January, the Chairman, William Whitelaw, was able to say: 'Four years ago seven pre-war Railway Companies became one in name and by Act of Parliament. To make them one in spirit has been not the least important task of the Directors and Management during this period. We had to start with seven traditions, seven loyalties, at least seven prejudices. . . . It is just because we have gone slowly in the scheme and development of our organisation . . . that we have reached a state in which I can without hesitation declare that we are already a Team. . . . Great Central engines have become a standard for Scotland . . . Great Northern permanent way will one day be our standard as it is our example, and both passenger and goods trains will run in England as punctually as they do now in Scotland . . .'

Nevertheless, despite new standard forms, throughout the 'twenties and for long after, it was immediately clear to the discerning traveller which of the pre-grouping companies' lines he was running over. The majority of the locomotives he saw were denizens of the locality. The coaches had easily recognisable differences of style denoting their previous ownership, nowhere more apparent than on the North Eastern, where the non-corridor, clerestory-roofed coaches designed by David Bain before he moved to the

Newcastle–Durham residential express. Four of David Bain's non-corridor clerestory-roofed coaches drawn by 3-cylinder 4-4-4 tank locomotive No 1328, a very elegant Raven design. Twenty were built 1913–14 and twenty-five between 1920 and 1922, but because they were deficient in adhesion and braking power, all were later converted to 4-6-2 by the LNER. At Chester Moor, County Durham, 17 August 1926.

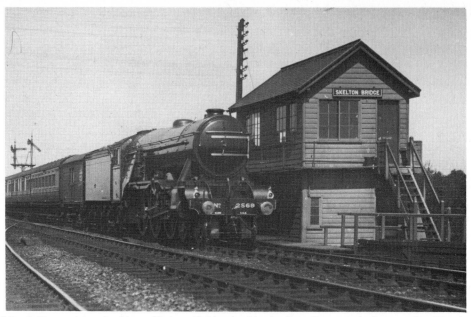

North Eastern signal cabin at Skelton Bridge beside the East Coast main line north of York. Well inland, this cabin needed no porch. No 2569 *Gladiateur* passing with an up express in May 1927.

North British signal box at Bridge of Earn, junction of the Fife coast line with the Edinburgh–Perth main line. Parts of the North British could also be draughty, hence the porch here. 5 July 1970.

Midland in 1903, predominated. Even signal boxes showed slight regional differences, most gabled but some with hipped roofs, and many of those on the North Eastern with a porch at the head of the steps to shield the inner door from keen east winds. Beside Great Northern tracks, he saw the distinctive 'somersault' signals, the arm balanced about a central pivot, which had been adopted after January 1876 when a signal arm of old fashioned type had frozen in the all-clear position with disastrous results.

Northwards and eastwards, engines standing at the head of a train puffed quietly and intermittently while the Westinghouse pump recharged the brake reservoirs, for Great Eastern, North Eastern, North British and Great North of Scotland★ all used this much more powerful braking system, so that it was a pity the LNER did not adopt it instead of falling into line with the other three groups in the use of the vacuum brake.

The regional styles of smaller stations remained little altered, not only through the quarter-century of LNER management, but until their wholesale slaughter under the Beeching axe. At the larger stations, there was seldom greater alteration than the appearance of new initials. The LNER built a new station at Welwyn Garden City in 1926, and in 1927 rebuilt the inadequate North British station at Berwick-on-Tweed with stone offices and an island platform, convenient for railway operation, though not so for passengers with hand baggage. The great stations were as individual as ever: the fine double-arched façade of King's Cross (1852) concealed a trainshed smoke-grimed by South Yorkshire coal; the heavy Victorian Gothic, brick-built, offices of the Great Eastern's Liverpool Street (1875) contrasted with elegant ironwork in the interior – when it could be seen through the smoke from the busy steam suburban trains; the pleasant brick and terra-cotta frontage of the Great Central's Marylebone (1899) screened a spacious concourse provided in anticipation that more platforms would be needed, but as they never were, it remained a clean and peaceful resort. Edinburgh Waverley had been impressively rebuilt by the North British in 1892–1902 with a vast island platform, spacious and light under a glazed ridge-and-furrow roof. But the two finest stations on the LNER, and two of the finest in Britain, were those of the North Eastern at Newcastle-upon-Tyne (1850) and York (1877), in each of which the trainshed, set on a curve and covered by glazed iron-arched roofs of three and four spans respectively, achieved a monumental splendour equalled only at Paddington. Newcastle was also graced by a fine façade, although never quite realising the ideal of

★ Although two histories of the LNER state that the GN of S was a 'vacuum' line, the two historians of that railway, H.A. Vallance and Sir Malcolm Barclay-Harvey, both record that it used the Westinghouse brake, and this is confirmed in pre-grouping issues of the Railway Year Book.

Pocklington station, York–Hull line, North Eastern Railway. A pleasing design in brick with stone facings by the York architect G.T. Andrews for the opening of the line in 1847. 27 August 1959.

The Pocklington stationmaster's house had a bay window looking out over the platform, and beside it was an ornate iron lamp bracket.

Newcastle Central station, busy on Saturday 29 August 1959.

Newcastle Central, the façade facing Neville Street. From an old postcard – cabs and trams, but not a sign of a motor-car!

the architect, John Dobson, which, it has been claimed, would have made it 'one of the finest 19th-century classical buildings in Europe'.*

This chapter is confined to the LNER as I knew it in the 'twenties. Yet to come was the company's enterprise of the 'thirties: widened lines, reconstructed stations, flying junctions, colour light signalling, new marshalling yards equipped with the latest methods of control, new Pacific locomotives of advanced design, streamlined pioneer high speed trains, new steamers for the Continental services.

★ *The Railway Heritage of Britain*, 1983, page 49.

CHAPTER THREE

AWAY TO THE NORTH-EAST

The LNER had a very effective scheme of management training, inherited from the North Eastern, and generally accepted as the best instituted by any British railway company. As both Cecil J. Allen and Michael Bonavia have pointed out, its success was proved after nationalisation by the remarkable number of former LNER men who were selected by the British Transport Commission to fill senior positions.

The scheme had been introduced by Sir George Gibb, General Manager of the North Eastern from 1891 to 1906, after he had been to the United States with some of his officers, and had returned convinced that changes must be made in the company's organisation, particularly in the traffic departments, and that well-educated and able young men must be recruited and trained for management. One of the first was R.L. Wedgwood, who was invited by Gibb to join the staff when he left Cambridge with a first-class degree in 1896 at the age of twenty-two. From this early beginning grew the Traffic Apprenticeship scheme, which, although intended primarily to attract university graduates, also took a few boys direct from public school and was open to promising young members of the clerical staff. All alike were expected to study diligently and pass examinations in railway subjects, but those from the clerical staff had also to sit an additional Traffic Apprentices' examination.

The basic educational facilities for clerical staff had been created by the North Eastern in the early years of the century with classes covering the rules and regulations governing block signalling and the safe working of trains, and in passenger and goods station working and accountancy, instruction in all three being given by railwaymen. In addition, there were advanced courses in railway operating, economics, law and geography, given by professors and lecturers from Armstrong College, Newcastle-upon-Tyne, and Leeds University. These could be attended in York, Leeds, Hull and Newcastle. Much could be learnt also from interesting and informative

45

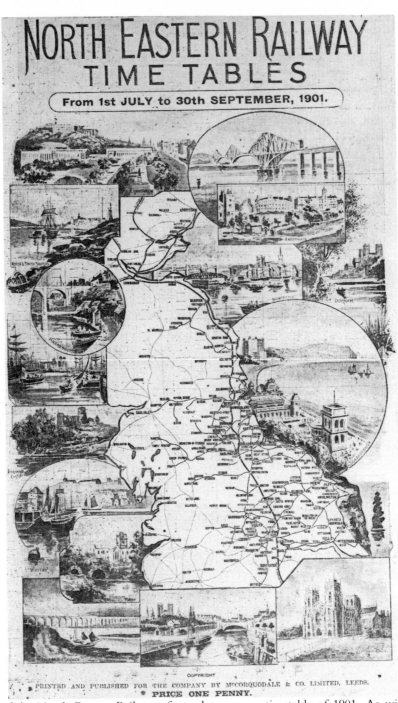

Map of the North Eastern Railway, from the summer timetable of 1901. As with most railway companies' timetable maps, this one shows many more lines than the North Eastern's own: the NE had running powers to Edinburgh, and regularly worked the East Coast expresses to that city, but all the lines north of Berwick on this map belonged to the North British. (*Photostat supplied by the National Railway Museum.*)

lectures which could be heard from time to time at such centres as the Railway Institute in York.

During their three years' training the apprentices were moved around every few months to gain experience on wayside stations, docks, and in district and head offices, and were summoned periodically to appear before a headquarters' Traffic Apprentices' Committee, even occasionally to submit a personal report on progress. Afterwards, there was further carefully planned movement from one post to another. This very thorough way of training prospective management personnel was organised for many years by the able hand, and watched over by the keen eye, of Robert Bell, the Assistant General Manager, who moved from York to King's Cross with Wedgwood.

After leaving school in the summer of 1924, I applied for a Traffic Apprenticeship and was later called to appear before the selection committee at King's Cross. Another applicant direct from school was selected, but not myself: after all, the LNER was primarily looking for graduates. As enquiries revealed that no one was ever given a second chance to appear before the selectors, that seemed to be final. But unknown to me, persistent probing of the high command was made on my behalf, and this eventually drew the information that just one way remained open: to join the clerical staff and work for the Traffic Apprentices' examination from within. This course being decided upon, I was summoned for two interviews at King's Cross. The first was with Sir Ralph Wedgwood himself, when I was impressed by his great personality, but, because of his understanding and the courtesy he showed to a youngster, not overawed; perhaps he remembered his own enthusiastic boyhood interest in railways.* The second was with Robert Bell, who, intense and direct, had not the same facility for setting one at ease. Both warned me that the way would be hard, but by no means impossible. These two busy and prestigious officers arranged the interviews for late in the evening, long after office hours, a time free from interruption; so I was able to make my way to King's Cross without asking my existing employers for permission to leave early, thereby perhaps arousing suspicion. A third visit, however, had to be made during the day to sit the examination incumbent upon all would-be entrants to the clerical staff: I forget what excuse I made for my absence, but it really no longer mattered, as the examination was unlikely to present any difficulty and departure would soon follow.

Three months later, I was told to report at York on 1 October – so I was to begin my railway service in the prestigious North Eastern Area. I was asked by what route I would travel so that a free pass could be issued for as much

---

* Cecil J. Allen in *The London & North Eastern Railway*, page 58, refers to Wedgwood's 'deep interest in, and affection for, railways and trains' from his early days.

47

of my journey as lay over LNER tracks. The Banbury route from Cheltenham was the obvious one, as well as the most convenient.

So on 30 September 1925, I boarded the Swansea–Newcastle express at Cheltenham South & Leckhampton. The train ambled up the formidable Cotswold escarpment to Andoversford and Notgrove, crossed over the Worcester line at Kingham, with frequent slowings to exchange one single line staff for another, before reaching Banbury, where I watched the Great Western 2-6-0 come off and the Great Central Atlantic take her place. The 'Jersey Lily' took us gently through Culworth Junction to the GC main line and toiled up through Woodford & Hinton to the summit at Charwelton before the pace increased on the descent through Catesby Tunnel; but with the frequent speed reductions over the reverse curves round the wide island platforms of each wayside station, and stops at Rugby, Leicester and Nottingham, the train was no flier. However, that did not lessen my enjoyment as I gazed through the window at the unfamiliar midlands scenery and the installations of a hitherto unknown railway – now 'my' railway! At Sheffield Victoria, the train reversed, a Robinson 4-4-0 coming on the rear and taking us through Rotherham, an unprepossessing area best seen at night (as I was to see it at Christmas), when the fiery furnaces of the steel works acquired an awesome grandeur. The sharply curved triangle at Mexborough led to the Swinton & Knottingley Joint Line (Midland and North Eastern), whence North Eastern tracks ran through Burton Salmon and Church Fenton to York.

Previously I had only seen photographs of York station; these, however, are but a pale reflection of the real thing. The graceful roof of arched spans supported by rows of cast iron columns, which seem as though to march in file round the curve, cannot fail to impress anyone possessed of sensitivity. Moreover, the station has an air of spaciousness, and even in the days of steam traction was surprisingly clean. Staying overnight in the lovely city, I reported, as bidden, the following morning to the area headquarters, that imposing, if slightly flamboyant, building erected by the North Eastern in 1906. There I learnt that my first posting was to Tynemouth goods station, and, furthermore, that there was a suitable train sometime after midday.

It was a York to Newcastle train, and I found it in a bay platform at the north end, headed by *Shotover*, a strange name to my eyes, unfamiliar as I was with winners of the St Leger and the Derby whose names had been aptly chosen for Gresley's breed of Pacifics. She had a surfeit of power for her light train, which itself gave me a surprise: there were first and third class dining cars gangwayed together in the middle of a set of David Bain's non-corridor clerestory coaches. Hence, if you wanted lunch, as I did, you took a seat in one of the cars and stayed there throughout the journey. This was an arrangement I had not previously met on other main line trains, in all of which the restaurant car could be reached from any part. But, as I was soon to realise, the North Eastern, so progressive in many ways, had no great

A 'Jersey Lily': Great Central Atlantic, class 8B designed by J.G. Robinson. No 264 was built by Beyer Peacock & Co. in 1904. From an old postcard.

Robinson 4-4-0 No 6027, class 11B, built by the Great Central at Gorton Works in 1902. The Scarborough–Sheffield express is a neat set of GC non-corridor coaches, seen at Chaloners Whin, south of York, on 3 September 1927.

North Eastern Railway headquarters in York, designed by architects Horace Field and William Bell and completed in 1906. Red brick with stone dressings, banded chimney stacks, a profusion of dormers, a tall pilastered entrance in the centre of the principal face, and an oriel window to the general manager's office below the flag pole on the near side. Easily criticised architecturally, but impressive and attractive when seen.

number of corridor coaches. Apart from the Anglo-Scottish trains formed with Pullman vestibuled East Coast Joint Stock, I can only recall fully connected NE sets running between Newcastle and Liverpool via Sunderland and Harrogate, Newcastle–York–Hull, and Leeds–York–Newcastle–Edinburgh–Glasgow, this last the most important of their trains and soon to be equipped with new LNER coaches. For the rest, the North Eastern was content to let the Midland provide corridor coaches for the Bristol–Newcastle workings, and the Lancashire & Yorkshire, Great Central, Great Western and London & South Western, the restaurant car trains running from Newcastle to Liverpool (via York), Swansea, Bournemouth, Southampton. There were spare North Eastern corridor coaches to be seen here and there, but relatively few in number, and as late as 1929 I saw non-corridors attached to strengthen the Leeds to Glasgow express which stopped only at Newcastle during the four hours' run between York and Edinburgh.

Nevertheless, there was evidence of North Eastern enterprise for me to watch out for as I travelled north. Between Alne and Thirsk, automatic signals had been installed in 1905 to increase line capacity. These used the

North Eastern corridor set on the Hull–Newcastle service crossing Scarborough Bridge over the River Ouse and passing under one of the great signal gantries at York station. 4-4-0 locomotive No 1239 of class R1, introduced in 1908. 11 May 1927.

Hall electro-gas system to operate pairs of semaphore arms on each post, home signal above, distant below, and through the wide window of the restaurant car I could see them bob up to the danger position when passed by the locomotive. There was, I think, no comparable system in use on any other main line in this country. It worked very successfully for many years before being superseded by colour-light signals.

After the stop at Darlington, I was on the look-out for the electrified line passing across near Aycliffe. This was then unique in Britain: overhead catenary wires were rare, electric locomotives rarer still, but long trains of mineral wagons hauled by large electric engines could be seen nowhere else in this country.

From Durham station, there was the superb view of cathedral and castle perched on the rocky peninsula in the loop of the River Wear, towering above the red roofs of the City. Smoky chimneys heralded the approach to Tyneside, and soon the train wound its way slowly on to the King Edward Bridge from which I saw the City of Newcastle-upon-Tyne rising steeply up the valley side from the river and, to my right, Robert Stephenson's High Level Bridge. Soon we came to rest in the splendid Central station.

There I saw more evidence of the old company's enterprise when I changed into the Tynemouth train. Three suburban routes had been electrified on the third rail 600 volt DC system in 1903–1904. Two of these formed a circle via Wallsend, Tynemouth, Whitley Bay, Backworth and

51

Newcastle–Liverpool express via Normanton, Rochdale and Manchester, in York station 11 July 1927. The Lancashire & Yorkshire 4-cylinder 4-6-0 No 1518, designed by G. Hughes, has taken over from a North Eastern locomotive. What would once have been an L & Y restaurant car set has become an LMS medley: Midland and LNWR 12-wheeled clerestory diners in the middle, and three other LNWR vehicles, can be seen among the seven.

Newcastle–South Wales express leaving York. Great Western Dean clerestory set. Great Central 4-4-0 No 6031 of class 11B. 4 October 1927.

Electric train from Tynemouth, North Eastern 1904 clerestory stock, approaching Newcastle Central station. The tracks crossing to the right lead to the High Level Bridge. Behind rises the great castle keep built for Henry II by Maurice the Engineer between 1168 and 1178. From an old postcard.

North Eastern 600 volt Bo–Bo electric locomotive, one of two built in 1904 to work the line to the Tyne Commission Quay, fitted to pick up current either from a third rail or from an overhead wire. Shown as restored in NER livery and exhibited in the National Railway Museum, by whom the photograph has been supplied.

Jesmond; the third was the Riverside line to Tynemouth via Walker, with stations serving the shipyards. I caught a tantalisingly brief glimpse of a small steeple-cab electric locomotive with a trolley pole drawing current from an overhead wire, like a tramcar;* this was a sight I was unprepared for, as I then knew nothing of the electrified line descending to the Tyne Commission Quay and passing through a tunnel where the little engine picked up electricity from a third rail instead of the wire. She worked for more than sixty years, long enough for her to survive and earn preservation in the National Railway Museum. My train followed the Riverside line, giving me a sight of the pioneer vessel *Turbinia* displayed in a cradle alongside the Parsons Steam Turbine Works, where she long remained until preserved under cover in Newcastle's Science Museum.

And so I came to Tynemouth, alighting in a clean, light station with ornate iron columns, platform canopies, wire floral baskets suspended from the roof girders; immaculately maintained and efficiently managed under the command of a tall and helpful stationmaster. Leaving my baggage, I went in search of somewhere to stay until I could find lodgings. The Bath Hotel proved willing in the off-season to meet the limitations of my pocket, so there I remained happily for a week until I found rooms with a widowed landlady known to one of the goods station staff, one of the kindest of souls who housed me well in a terrace house in Mariners Lane, an appropriate name in that seafaring area.

Tynemouth goods station, now closed, was a stately little Tudor style stone building, two-storeyed, with a projecting portico, above which the goods agent's room looked out through a mullioned oriel. Obviously it had not been built for its existing use; it had, in fact, been the terminus of the Newcastle & North Shields Railway from 1847 until 1882, when the opening of the coast line via Whitley Bay made a new station necessary. The goods station handled much fish as well as general merchandise, and there I was effectually office-boy, licker-on of stamps, and typist of such letters as were not hand-written above a carbon paper. Having no previous experience of typewriters, I learnt the hard way, with the result that touch-typing remains a craft mystery hidden from me to this day. The goods agent was a kindly man, and as Northumberland was near enough to the Border to celebrate New Year's Day in addition to the English Christmas Bank Holidays, he let me spend an extra day at home over Christmas on condition that I formed one of the skeleton staff manning the goods station on 1 January.

Tynemouth – 'Tinmouth' in Northumberland, but when talking to friends further south, I had to be careful lest I gave quite the wrong impression geographically – was a very pleasant town to be in. There was

* Does memory play me false? There seems some doubt whether she ever had a trolley pole, collecting through a pantograph instead, as shown in the photograph.

Tynemouth goods station. Built in 1847 as the terminus of the Newcastle & North Shields Railway, it became the goods station when the new passenger station was built in 1882. Photograph, taken in July 1981, kindly supplied by Colin Alexander.

North Pier reaching out from Tynemouth, protecting the entry to the River Tyne. 28 August 1959.

one wide main shopping street, and on the great headland dominating the town, a fortress then still a military stronghold, the remnants of a medieval castle, and a ruined priory where beautiful workmanship survived. The long North Pier, built with huge blocks of masonry, stretched out into the North Sea, protecting, with the even longer South Pier reaching out from South Shields, the entry to the Tyne. At the root of the breakwater stood the mason's yard, an intriguing spot where cyclopian blocks of unused ashlar lay among massive timber-framed bogies and grass-grown rails converging to a single track running out along the pier to the lighthouse.

The splendours of the Northumbrian coast lie far to the north of Tynemouth, but there were pleasant walks at hand. My favourite was along the sea front through Cullercoats and Whitley Bay to Holywell Dene, a pretty spot deep out-of-sight of the coalpits. Sometimes I went further along the coast to Seaton Sluice and thence inland to Seaton Delaval: I well remember my first astonished sight of the vast empty Hall of the Delavals, fire-blackened, designed early in the eighteenth century by Sir John Vanbrugh, of whose Baroque architecture I then knew nothing. Southward, I could cross the river by ferry into County Durham and walk along the coastal path to Marsden Rocks and the Lizard Point lighthouse, seeing on the way an ancient locomotive hauling even more ancient four-wheeled carriages, former Great North of Scotland vehicles acquired by the South Shields Marsden & Whitburn Colliery Railway after the Centenary Celebrations that summer. In evenings, seeking air and exercise after office hours, I would walk out along the breakwater, taking a delight on stormy days in dodging the clouds of spray flying over the parapet.

I have always retained an affection for Tynemouth, and in October 1925 I expected to be left there in comparative obscurity while I studied for the railway company's examinations. Three evenings a week I travelled into Newcastle to attend the lectures given by railway staff on accountancy and signalling. I looked forward to the spring and summer months, with better light for photography and longer days when one would be able to go further afield.

But that was not to be, so the intended photographs of the electric trains, especially the workmen's set of small elderly carriages hauled by a motor parcels van, and of the South Shields Marsden & Whitburn Colliery Railway, were never taken.

CHAPTER FOUR

WAYSIDE STATION

In years gone by, the railway station was a lively part of village life, a source of useful information, not least the answer to who came, who went. There were the regular passengers, long distance travellers, locals off for a day's shopping, day trippers, school children; and beyond the platforms was the goods yard into which farmers drove their carts and wagons and herded cattle for entrainment. It was also a microcosm of railway life, and, as such, the favourite training ground for new entrants to the service. The accepted code was that passengers and customers should be helped and encouraged to the best of one's ability, and that every effort should be made to run the trains punctually.

My own postings were to two stations in County Durham and one in the East Riding of Yorkshire. The first, to which I was sent towards the end of January 1926 after four months at Tynemouth, was Hylton on the now abandoned line between Sunderland and Durham. The principal settlement was South Hylton, which had coalesced on the bank of the River Wear where there was a quay and a vehicle ferry that, until the river was bridged at Sunderland in 1796, had been a link in the main road between that town and Newcastle. Encouraged, no doubt, by the opening of the railway in 1853 and the growth of local industry, rows of cottages had spread up the slope from the river as far as the railway station, but the old part was still picturesque although the flowing water was heavily polluted. North Hylton, backed by hanging woods on the steep flank of the valley, was very small.

Hylton is some three miles west of Sunderland, still in 1926 separated from the town by green fields, and as it lay well beyond the tram terminus, the railway carried a modest commuter traffic. Goods traffic was considerable, as there were wire works and a large flourishing paper mill, each served by private sidings. The tracks were also used by the Lambton Hetton & Joicey Collieries between the sidings of their private railways near

Hylton station, County Durham, on the Sunderland–Durham branch. Looking to the signal cabin and level crossing on 13 April 1926.

Penshaw, and Pallion, on their way to the Lambton and Hetton staithes just above the Wear bridges. North Eastern locomotives were well kept in the 'twenties, but they were outshone by the engines heading the LHJC coal tains, for those, however elderly, were immaculately maintained in their green livery, richly lined-out.

Augmented by the coal trains, traffic passed day and night, and the signal cabin (for the North Eastern Railway had signal 'cabins', not 'boxes') alongside the level crossing was manned by three signalmen in turn, 6 a.m. to 2 p.m., 2 p.m. to 10 p.m., and 10 p.m. to 6 a.m. Other staff were a stationmaster, senior clerk, second clerk, two lad porters who worked shifts on the platforms, and a goods porter who spent much of his time at the paper mill sidings, sheeting wagons with the heavy tarpaulins, recording the outgoing bales of paper and the incoming wagon-loads of esparto grass from Sunderland Docks, for it was at the Ford Paper Works, opened in 1838, that the use of esparto grass in paper making had been developed.

I had some difficulty finding accommodation in the village, preferring to be on the spot rather than lodge in Sunderland, and it was a day or two before I was accepted in a house in Primrose Street where I was well-fed and comfortable, though a hip-bath had to serve in the absence of a bathroom.

Three evenings a week I continued to travel to Newcastle for the railway company's classes, and as it had already become clear that operating methods appealed to me far more than accountancy, I hoped for practical instruction in the cabin when off duty. Furthermore, as an alternative to shorthand, I had to learn to use the single-needle telegraph. This was an archaic system, introduced in the 1850s and deriving from the earliest use of the telegraph on the Great Western in 1839. Although the signal cabins were linked by telephone, all written orders and messages were necessarily transmitted by the telegraph instrument, and as the signalmen operated that, there was only one place in which I could be taught.

Visits to the cabin were at first tentative, but I was made welcome and soon a close friendship with the three men built up. Two of them were Yorkshiremen, and all three, although very different, were men of sterling character: Doug Owston, Sam Watson and Matt Wilson of cherished memory. They were very patient, but I was not an apt pupil – my ear never responded quickly to the 'ting' and 'tang' as the telegraph needle swung from side to side, striking first one and then the other of two metal strips as it spelt out the letters. One Sunday evening when traffic was light, the signalman manning the next cabin, hearing the slow beats and guessing what was afoot, joined in until he realised that his thoughtful intervention was getting nowhere. Eventually I passed a test, but I have always thought that the examiners in the telegraph office on Newcastle Central station must have been very lenient.

The lad porters, who were frequent visitors to the cabin, were, of course, only four or five years younger than myself. One, a Geordie boy of character and integrity named Bob, came from a home in one of the poorer quarters of Sunderland, but differences of background were of little moment, and when he was off work for a long period, threatened with tuberculosis, and I went several times to see him, I was always welcomed warmly by his mother as well as by himself. His place was filled temporarily by a relief, a strong powerfully built boy, another Bob and another fine character, who lodged in the village and therefore often joined the evening sessions in the signal cabin, where by no means all the time was devoted to telegraphy. There was opportunity for both of us to learn the block signalling system and to send, under strict supervision, the bell-signals exchanged with the next cabin, signifying the type of train approaching, whether the section ahead was clear for its passage, its entry to the Hylton section, and finally its exit, each freight train watched closely to make sure that the last vehicle carried a tail-lamp, proving that no part of it had broken away. Meantime, the crossing-gates had to be opened and the signals lowered and replaced in proper sequence; there is a knack in pulling signal levers against the tension of wires or the resistance of point-rodding, by placing a foot upon the frame and throwing one's weight backwards, a knack soon mastered by that stalwart lad.

In the intervals between trains, we discussed railway matters and the affairs of the world in general. One evening, after the night duty man had taken over, the afternoon one stayed on, and we continued so long that the

Durham–Sunderland train about to stop at Hylton. North Eastern 2-4-2 tank locomotive No 1578 of a class introduced by T.W. Worsdell in 1886. 15 April 1926.

Train from Sunderland to Durham and Bishop Auckland approaching Hylton, drawn by 2-4-0 No 1470 of the very successful 1463 class, designed in 1885 by a committee of divisional locomotive superintendents under General Manager Henry Tennant, after the resignation of the unpopular locomotive superintendent, Alexander McDonnell. 27 August 1926.

Sunderland–Durham train approaching Hylton. The coaches were of an 1899 design with low elliptical roofs and 'birdcage' lookouts for the guard. 4-4-0 No 217 had been rebuilt by Wilson Worsdell in 1901 from a 2-4-0 of his brother's, T.W. Wordsell's, design. 16 April 1926.

Sunday half-day excursion from Newcastle and Sunderland to York and Scarborough, calling to pick up at Hylton. Class S3 4-6-0 mixed traffic engine No 1374. 29 August 1926.

lad was locked out of his lodgings and spent the night on a settee in mine. It was the spring of 1926, so the threatened General Strike was a frequent topic. None of the railwaymen I knew wanted to take part, knowing full well that closure of the railways drives traffic to the roads. They also knew that union officials were too often demagogues, unrepresentative of the majority. Nevertheless, loyalty held them to their union's orders. I respected their position, and they respected mine as a probationer who must remain at work or lose his place. Only one, the senior clerk, a shifty individual, withheld this recognition, threatening that I would have to do as others did; predictably, when the strike came he ignored his union's call and spent the time working in a signal cabin elsewhere – a 'blackleg' if ever there was one.

Trains were of great variety. The LHJC coal trains came behind elderly 0-6-0 tender engines and more recent 0-6-2 tanks. The North Eastern locals, some of which ran through to Bishop Auckland, and the one or two expresses between Sunderland and Durham, were hauled by 0-4-4 and 2-4-2 tanks and 2-4-0 and 4-4-0 tender engines. There were a few fast freight trains drawn by Sir Vincent Raven's three-cylinder 4-6-0 mixed traffic loco-motives, and the daily 'pick up' goods whose 0-6-0 shunted wagons in and out of the goods yard and the private sidings. A curiosity was the Stores Train, a rake of vans which turned up periodically with supplies of lamp-oil, ropes, paper and miscellaneous hardware. Exceptionally there were out-of-gauge loads, massive pieces of industrial equipment of the kind that now moves on low-loaders accompanied by police escort. Those I saw passing through Hylton were bed-plates for ships' engines, cast in a foundry at Tyne Dock and carried to Doxford's, diesel engine builders at Pallion. Each bed-plate was 15 feet 8 inches wide, and, loaded on a sixty-ton twelve-wheeled flat wagon, overhung by 5 feet 8 inches on one side and one foot on the other. Necessarily, such a load could only be transported on a Sunday when the adjacent track could be kept clear. Start and finish were not far apart, but because a load of this width could not pass through Sunderland station, a roundabout route had to be used, the train reversing twice and travelling part of the way on the facing track, nowhere exceeding a speed of 10 mph.

Quite a number of special passenger trains used the line through Hylton, which was classed as suitable for even the heaviest locomotives, so that one Saturday I saw the three-cylinder Gresley Pacific *Shotover* come roaring up the grade from Sunderland with a football special, the off-beat exhaust from her inside cylinder emphasising its greater share of the work. On summer Sundays, Raven's mixed traffic engines brought excursion trains from Newcastle and Sunderland to York and Scarborough, stopping to pick up passengers from Hylton. It was one such that met with tragic disaster at Darlington two years later, when it struck head-on a locomotive which had passed beyond shunting limits. Twenty-five people were killed and forty-five seriously injured, many of them from Hylton, the loss of young and old long casting a shadow over so small a community.

62

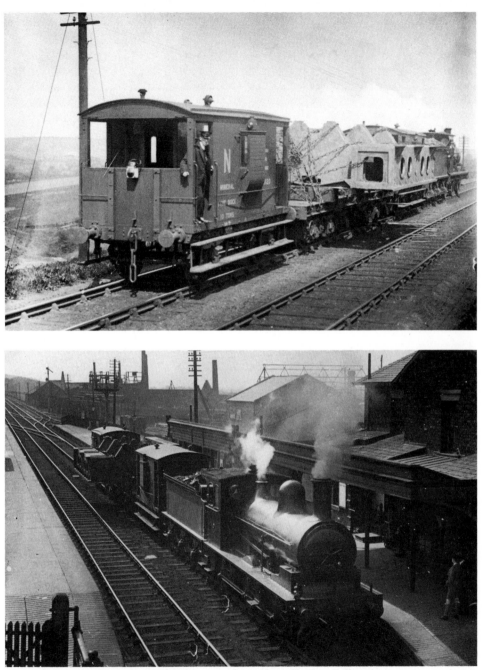

Out-of-gauge loads passing Hylton en route from Tyne Dock to Pallion by a circuitous route, in each case conveying a bedplate for ships' engines on a 60-ton 12-wheeled wagon. Photographed from the signal cabin on Sundays 11 April and 2 May 1926.

Class A express goods from Darlington to Tyne Dock passing Hylton. North Eastern 3-cylinder 4-6-0 No 943, class S3 designed by Sir Vincent Raven and introduced in 1919. 13 April 1926.

A rare bird! The North Eastern Area Stores Train arriving at Hylton behind 0-4-4 tank No 1788, designed by Wilson Worsdell and built in 1894. 2 June 1926.

Towards the end of June, I was moved to Usworth, a station serving a mining village on what had once been part of the East Coast main line southward from Newcastle, but which today carries only freight trains. It was two miles from Hylton as the crow flies, but by road over Biddick Bridge about 8½ miles. Nevertheless, I decided to stay on in my Hylton lodgings. Under the Washington stationmaster, who paid us daily visits, the two Usworth clerks worked alternate Sundays and daily shifts, 6 a.m. to 2 p.m. and 2 p.m. to 10 p.m., so morning and night there was no other transport to or from the station but one's own. It was high summer, so an early morning walk of just over two miles, crossing the river by the Hylton ferry, had its attractions. Peace and beauty lay upon the fields above the Wear, but even the splendour of the sunrise must fade, and the motor-bicycle soon came into its own. The road by Biddick Bridge passed Washington Old Hall, an early seventeenth-century sandstone building incorporating the great hall of a medieval manor which had been the home of George Washington's ancestors; it seemed strangely out-of-place in such surroundings, yet, although divided into tenements, sadly neglected and threatened with demolition, it retained an air of faded dignity. Years later, I was glad to learn it had been saved, restored by American generosity, and placed in the care of the National Trust.

At both stations there were tickets to be collected, and in my early days at Hylton the contract ticket holders, assuming recognition, only grudgingly complied with my request to show their passes. Twice, a bewildered schoolboy arrived, having boarded the wrong train, and, without enough cash to get him home, had to ask for a loan. My colleagues in the Hylton office remarked derisively that I would never see that half-crown again: they were wrong, as a Postal Order came only a few days later. At Usworth, the boy came in person with his coin and his thanks, brought by his grateful father by car.

Shift working – no one then talked of 'unsocial hours' – meant that there were long summer afternoons which could be spent photographing trains on the east coast main line near Durham. With the help of the one-inch Ordnance Survey map and the motor-cycle, I made several forays before finding two ideal sites: at Chester Moor where southbound trains were bathed in brilliant light; and further south at Hett Mill, near Ferryhill, where the sinuous course of the main line swept northbound trains into a similar angle with the afternoon sun. Often of course, something tempting appeared running in the opposite direction so that the front end was heavily in shadow, but it was at these two sites that I took what I have always felt to be my finest railway photographs.

The third wayside station, to which I was sent at the beginning of 1927 after an interlude at Kingston-upon-Hull, was far more of a 'country' station than the other two. Some twenty-odd miles west of that City, it stood in the flat lands reclaimed from marshes once washed by the tidal River Ouse.

Usworth station, County Durham, Newcastle–Pelaw–Leamside–Ferryhill line, which was part of the East Coast main line from 1850 to 1872. The porch at the head of the steps to the signal cabin shows up clearly. 21 August 1926.

Victoria bridge, River Wear, Washington, built 1838 for the Durham Junction Railway, and from 1850 to 1872 forming part of the NER East Coast main line. A particularly graceful viaduct with four wide arches, and three narrow ones on each side. From a card postmarked 1910.

Early morning Sunday train from York to Newcastle via Leamside arriving at Usworth behind North Eastern 3-cylinder Pacific No 2403 *City of Durham*, 29 August 1926. The five City class engines were Raven's riposte to Gresley's Great Northern Pacifics, but they never achieved the same reputation.

Class C goods passing Usworth behind 3-cylinder 0-8-0 No 633, class T3 introduced by Raven in 1919. 28 August 1926.

North Eastern class P3 0-6-0 No 1205, built by Beyer Peacock & Co. in 1908, shunting the pick-up goods at Usworth, 21 August 1926. Class P3, of which 115 were built, was introduced by Wilson Worsdell in 1906.

North Eastern 0-8-0 of class T with the pick-up goods at Usworth in the summer of 1926. Class T was designed by Wilson Worsdell, and ninety were built, with variations, between 1901 and 1904.

Serving the village of Laxton, but taking its name from the county family at the Hall whose ancestors had held the manor in the thirteenth century, Saltmarshe station is on the main line from Hull through Goole to Doncaster and so King's Cross. It was manned by a stationmaster, one clerk, two lad porters, and six signalmen, three taking shifts in the station cabin, the other three perched atop the girders of Skelton Swing Bridge across the Ouse. Roads were few and lanes were muddy in that U-shaped, river-girt loop of land, so the railway was a lifeline to the village of Laxton and surrounding farms, as at the time of writing it still is; it may not be such for much longer, however, because Skelton Bridge, several times damaged by passing ships, is in need of repair or replacement at a heavy cost British Rail is unwilling to meet.

The stationmaster and I shared the office work. He knew well how to train anyone sent to his station, for he dealt with any mistake in a firm but kindly manner; and as he trusted his staff, the atmosphere was a happy one. Before I arrived, he had already found lodgings for me in a four-roomed cottage where I was well cared for by an elderly couple; but an attack of 'flu while enveloped in a feather mattress is not to be recommended! A friendly man with an endless repertoire of stories, not all of them bearing on railway life, he proved an entertaining companion. But there was not Hylton's camaraderie with the signalmen – neither when I visited the station cabin, nor when I climbed to that on the swing bridge to see the intricate arrangements safeguarding its operation, was I well received. Undoubtedly, this derived from one man, a left-wing blusterer. During the General Strike the previous May, he had brought in the NUR branch secretary in an attempt to dussuade the stationmaster from working the line, and failing in that, had threatened to throw him our of the cabin. Had he tried to mount the steps, his descent would certainly have been sudden.

Of the two lad porters, one was a dark haired country boy of eighteen, bearing the euphonious old Anglo-Saxon name of Alwyn, too fine a name for common use so known to us as Tom. He had joined the railway on leaving school, and had developed into a very reliable worker, willing and ready to turn his hand to anything, never out of temper. The other, George, was not quite sixteen, son of one of the signalmen. At the date of the strike, he had still been a probationer, so although his father obeyed the union's orders, he had had to persuade his son to stay at work, a difficult positon which failed to arouse the left-wing man's sympathy. George was shy and diffident, and had been easy prey for the nagging tongue of my predecessor, so although Tom's friendship was soon assured, George's was withheld.

Though country station work was often easy, the small staff was under pressure at times, particularly when half the village thronged the office just before departure time of the train to the neighbouring market town of Goole, all wanting tickets, one with a parcel to be weighed and charged, and vehemently indignant because it had to be left for another train. There were

Skelton Swing Bridge, River Ouse, between Saltmarshe and Goole, was opened in 1869, completing the direct route from Doncaster to Hull. It was then the second largest of the kind in the world. The centre span, 250 feet long and weighing 670 tons, was hydraulically worked, rotating on a turntable 30 feet in diameter. The five fixed plate-girder spans were each 116 feet long. (*Photograph: National Railway Museum.*)

Monkwearmouth Bridge, Sunderland, on a Sunday in March 1926 during tests by the Bridge Stress Committee to measure deflection and the effect of 'hammer-blow' caused by the reciprocating parts of a steam locomotive. Monkwearmouth was one of 52 bridges examined, and the favourite locomotives, noted for developing exceptionally large vibration, were Lancashire & Yorkshire 0–8–0 No 1438 and Great Central Atlantic No 5360. No 1438 is one of the two leading engines, and No 5360 is the fourth. Note the elegant ironwork of the cross-member between the main girders of the bridge, which was designed by T.E. Harrison, Chief Engineer of the NER, and completed in 1879. (*Reproduced by kind permission of the Newcastle Chronicle & Journal.*)

constant interruptions to routine paperwork: a passenger wanted to know the route for a complicated journey; the need to record a wagon number on an invoice meant leaving the office, locking it, and visiting the goods yard; a churn of milk once arrived as the train steamed in, so parcels stamps had to be hurriedly stuck to the label and the label tied to the churn in the van as the train began to move. Once a whistle was blown violently from the signal cabin, and a lad porter came rushing into the office, saying the signalman had received the 'Stop and Examine' bell-code, and was about to halt an express on which an open door had been observed. Had someone fallen out? Traffic on the opposite line was halted, and when the train drew in, it was for us to board it and make enquiries. The guard had noticed nothing amiss. Surprised passengers assured us that no one was missing from the compartment; so there was no occasion for further delay, but the driver of the next train in the opposite direction was warned to be specially alert.

This was very small beer. Not so, however, at Hull on the morning of 14 February 1927. To us at Saltmarshe, there came from Paragon station a telegram whose words I remember clearly: 'All trains running late. Collision here.' How serious it was, of course we did not know, and when the Hull–King's Cross express passed through not unduly behind its scheduled time, we hoped for the best. Not until the first stopping train called did we hear news of a disaster. An outgoing train to Scarborough had been correctly signalled, but a relief signalman, enjoined to avoid delay to the approaching morning business train from Withernsea, put the signal to danger as soon as the Scarborough engine had passed but before it had reached the points which that signal protected. It ought not to have been possible to reverse those points until the outgoing train had cleared them, but a gap in the locking system enabled a second signalman to do so inadvertently, diverting the Scarborough train into the path of that from Withernsea. Twelve passengers were killed and twenty-four badly injured, many of them businessmen who regularly travelled together in the six-wheeled Withernsea Club Saloon, a vehicle so small and light that it was smashed to matchwood by the impact.

The trains seen at Saltmarshe were of greater variety than at Hylton, for this was a section of the North Eastern over which two pre-grouping companies had running powers to Hull. Lancashire & Yorkshire trains used it from Goole, expresses drawn by Aspinall's Atlantics, freight trains behind massive 0–8–0s. Great Central freight and passenger trains came from Liverpool via Sheffield and Doncaster, one of them an express pulled by a four-cylinder mixed traffic 4-6-0 with a through coach off the Swansea–Newcastle train which I knew so well. I promised myself interesting photographs when the light grew stronger.

When I was transferred to Saltmarshe, I was half way through one of the advanced educational courses, Railway Operating, given by a professor from Newcastle, a series I found of the greatest interest. It was easy enough to reach Hull, but there was no train back to any station nearer than Staddlethorpe (now Gilberdyke), all of 6½ miles away by road and muddy lane through the darkness, or 3¾ miles along straight railway track. Stepping from sleeper to sleeper facing oncoming traffic is safe enough, but although there were few trains in the late evening, I always had to get out of the way of the King's Cross–Hull express, not by stepping across to the adjoining track and incurring the risk of being trapped by another train, but by scrambling down the side of the low embankment when I saw her headlamps approaching; then there was a roar, a fiery glare from the footplate, a rush of lighted windows, a gleam of green from the shaded table lamps of the dining car, and she was gone. There were moonlight nights when I made good progress, but there were others when wind and rain swept keenly across the marshes, and, worst of all, nights of fog when ears were strained to catch every sound. It was not altogether enjoyable, and I was always very glad when the lights of the Saltmarshe signals became visible. Twice I was lucky enough to find a freight train held at the junction, manned by an obliging crew who let me travel with them on the footplate. One of those occasions was a night of bitter frost when the driver of the big L&Y 0-8-0 insisted on bringing his train almost to a stop, and his fireman leant over the side of the cab, watchful and concerned lest I should slip on the icy platform.

My days at Saltmarshe were some of the happiest of my life. I loved living in a village, walking at weekends in the empty and unspoilt countryside, glorying in the gaunt splendour of bare trees silhouetted against frost-bound fields reaching to a far horizon.

However, my sojourn there was short, for after little more than nine weeks I was called to an assignment in York. So I bade farewell to my good friends at the station, and, as at Tynemouth, departed with intentions unfulfilled; but though I took no photographs, I had recorded many impressions.

Up afternoon Scotsman behind Raven Pacific No 2402 *City of York*, one of the three later members of the class completed with outside axle boxes to the trailing wheels. At Chester Moor, 17 August 1926. Chester Moor is beside the Team Valley line opened in 1868 from Gateshead to Durham City, which, after the completion of the line south to Ferryhill in 1872, formed part of the East Coast main line.

Up Sunday Scotsman at Chester Moor, drawn by a pair of Atlantics, 22 August 1926. The North Eastern, like the Great Western and the Great Northern, was averse to double-heading, but if the regular set of coaches was strengthened by extra vehicles and no Pacific was available, piloting could not be avoided. Here class Z No 719 leads No 698 (of Wilson Worsdell's 2-cylinder class V1, 1911) on a train with four extras, including, as Sunday trains then often did, a van carrying scenery for a theatrical company.

Class Z No 735 with a Newcastle–Darlington train. The three horse boxes suggest a race meeting somwhere in the neighbourhood. 17 August 1926.

The Aberdeen–King's Cross Express Meat Train behind class V No 532, the first North Eastern Atlantic, built to Wilson Worsdell's design with 6ft 10in driving whels in 1903. The train of vans, fitted throughout with continuous brakes, ran three times a week, and, leaving Aberdeen at 10.40 a.m. and scheduled to complete the journey in 12½ hours, travelled at speeds little less than those of the contemporary express passenger trains. Chester Moor, 17 August 1926.

No 2212, here seen on the down afternoon Scotsman at Chester Moor, was unique. The last of class Z, built at Darlington in 1917, she had her three cylinders on the Uniflow principle, and the sound of her exhaust was quite distinctive. 2 June 1926.

Down Harrogate Pullman hurried along by class Z Atlantic No 2196, 17 August 1926, when the Pullman was running non-stop from King's Cross to Harrogate via Church Fenton, and on through Northallerton to Newcastle and Edinburgh, but had yet to receive the title *Queen of Scots*, bstowed near the end of 1927.

Up Class A express freight, 3-cylinder class S3 4-6-0 No 923, in the late evening of 2 June 1926.

This was followed at 7.20 p.m. by the Night Mail, which, during the prolonged mining dispute in 1926, combined the 7 p.m. Newcastle–Bristol and Newcastle–London mail trains; a heavy load for Raven's first Pacific of 1922, No 2400 *City of Newcastle*, which had inside bearings for the trailing wheels.

Down class A express freight drawn by Gresley 3-cylinder 2-6-0 No 17, built at Darlington, the first of a modified version of his Great Northern design, having shortened chimneys and North Eastern type cabs. As none of the standard tenders was ready in time, she was temporarily atttached to one of GN make. At Chester Moor, 2 June 1926.

Up express fish train behind class Z No 2200. The first twenty of the class were built by the North British Locomotive Co. in 1911. A further twenty were added in 1918. At Chester Moor, 2 June 1926.

Up afternoon Scotsman at Hett, between Ferryhill and Durham City, on the last section completing a direct route for the East Coast main line from Doncaster to Newcastle. It was opened in 1872 from Tursdale Junction to the intricate weave of junctions at Relly Mill, a mile south-west of Durham City, where it converged with tracks from Bishop Auckland, Waterhouses, and Consett (via Lanchester). Behind the two leading coaches and No 2571 *Sunstar*, is the triplet articulated restaurant car. Here at Hett, the railway followed the valley of a tributary of the River Wear in a beautiful setting. 18 August 1926.

Up express with class Z No 2195 evidently fired by poor quality coal owing to the mining dispute. 29 May 1926.

Down afternoon Scotsman at speed behind No 2562 *Isinglass* – an odd name for a racehorse and a locomotive! 29 May 1926.

Down Harrogate Pullman running fast behind class Z No 2196. 18 August 1926.

Up parcels, LNWR and GNR bogie vans between NE 6-wheeled vans. Class Z No 2208. 29 May 1926.

The up parcels train, again with LNWR and GNR bogie vans (fifth and sixth) among a mixture of NE vehicles, the leading one of the unattractive straight-sided 1907 style. The handsome locomotive, No 1206, is one of a Wilson Worsdell's very successful class R, introduced in 1899. At Hett, 18 August 1926.

Down goods hauled by 0–6–0 No 1338, class C, most of which had been converted by Wilson Worsdell from 2-cylinder compounds built by his brother, T.W. Worsdell, from 1886 onwards. Passing Hett Mill signal cabin on 3 September 1926.

Down express goods passing Hett Mill signal cabin behind class S 4–6–0 No 753, a modified version of Wilson Worsdell's express passenger type of 1899. 3 September 1926.

CHAPTER FIVE

INTERLUDES
THE GENERAL STRIKE – HULL DOCKS

The General Strike, called for the beginning of May 1926 by the Trades Union Congress in futile support of the miners, cut all normal methods of communication between district offices and the stations and depots under their control. The offices therefore called for volunteers owning their own transport, those with cars taking men to work, those with motor-bicycles acting as despatch riders carrying letters, notices and posters for public display to the supervisory staff who remained at work. So my motor-bicycle and I reported to the District Superintendent's Office in Sunderland.

During the first few days all was quiet, and we sped peacefully from station to station in the northern parts of County Durham, welcomed by stationmasters who looked to us for news (for some days there were no newspapers) as well as official instructions, and were liberal with refreshments as we talked. Sometimes we had to stop to ask our way from little knots of men, who, perhaps mistaking us for despatch riders on union business, readily gave us the help we needed. But very soon pickets appeared, union messengers wore armbands, company's riders became known by sight, and there were unpleasant incidents. One rider found his tyres slashed when he came out of a station, others were driven off.

It was all very mild compared with the violent scenes enacted in more recent disputes, but nevertheless it was decided that thenceforward despatch riders should go in pairs instead of singly, so that one man could stand by the machines while the other delivered the messages. Roads followed on the outward journey were to be avoided on return. Consett, the iron smelting town on the eastern edge of the Pennines high above the valley of the Derwent, soon gained an unfortunate reputation, strikers overturning a bus one evening and threatening that nothing on wheels would be allowed into the town next day. So three of us, there being an odd man left when the rest had paired, took the precaution of stopping a mile from the town, and while two remained as though tending the machines, the third shed his motoring kit and walked to the station. But the strikers' threat proved an idle one, for he found all as peaceful as could be; and two days later other messengers, riding direct to the station, found a good humoured crowd gathered on the bridge over the tracks, laughing at the efforts of volunteers to swing a locomotive on the turntable. Indeed, most of our rides were no more than pleasant country excursions.

Amateurs did nobly, handling barrows on platforms, renewing signal lamps, travelling in the vans of passenger and freight trains to act as porters at each station, tackling, usually in pairs, the arduous task of firing a locomotive. Passengers waiting for a connecting train were known to spend the time sweeping the platform. Stationmasters manned the signal cabins, hoping, after long unfamiliarity, they had set the points correctly for a shunting goods train, opening crossing-gates for a passenger train, leaving road transport fuming while they handled parcels and collected tickets. Drivers, necessarily, had to have some knowledge of steam locomotives and signalling; I well remember being on a station on the East Coast main line when the first express train from the south came through, driven by an engineer who was leaning out of the cab, obviously enjoying himself, as did many less qualified than he for the work they undertook.

The one really serious incident in the north-east, the worst during the entire strike and without parallel in any other part of Britain, was not caused by industrial workers, still less by railwaymen who would never have countenanced such a deed, but by miners. Loosening a rail at Cramlington, north of Newcastle, they derailed an Anglo-Scottish express. The fireman and two passengers were injured, but the outcome would have been far more serious if the driver had not been proceeding cautiously after being warned that criminal damage to the track was suspected.

My own most vivid recollections of the strike are, however, of two unexpected acts of kindness. One occurred while I was riding through Durham City. It was a wide road with sloping grass banks on either side and houses set back above. As I passed, a small child ran down the bank on my left, heading straight into my path. All I could do was to tilt over to my right so that the child would hit, instead of being hit by, the front wheel. Both of us shaken but unharmed, and the child in tears, we got up, and when I raised the machine I found no damage other than a bent footrest. Meantime, figures had appeared in doorways, and one of them, an elderly lady, came forward and invited me in for a cup of tea. Inside I could not go, because I knew that my companion would soon return to find me. When he did so, he found me seated on the curb, drinking tea, surrounded by a friendly little group, all assuring me I was in no way to blame for the accident; but it might have been very different.

The second kind action was that of one of my friends at Hylton. My

The General Strike, 1926. Volunteers handling parcels traffic on Newcastle Central station. (*Reproduced by kind permission of the Newcastle Chronicle & Journal Ltd.*)

A volunteer inserting a fresh lamp on a signal gantry at Newcastle. The lower, smaller semaphore is a 'Calling-on' arm, a type the North Eastern was particularly addicted to, permitting limited shunting movement when the upper arm was at danger. (*Newcastle Journal.*)

The Anglo-Scottish express derailed by miners at Cramlington, Northumberland, on 10 May 1926. No 2565 *Merry Hampton* up against a brick wall. (*Newcastle Journal.*)

Cramlington. The twisted body of a coach up against the restaurant car which is perched over the edge of an embankment. But for the Buckeye couplers and Pullman gangways, the destruction would have been far greater. (*Newcastle Journal.*)

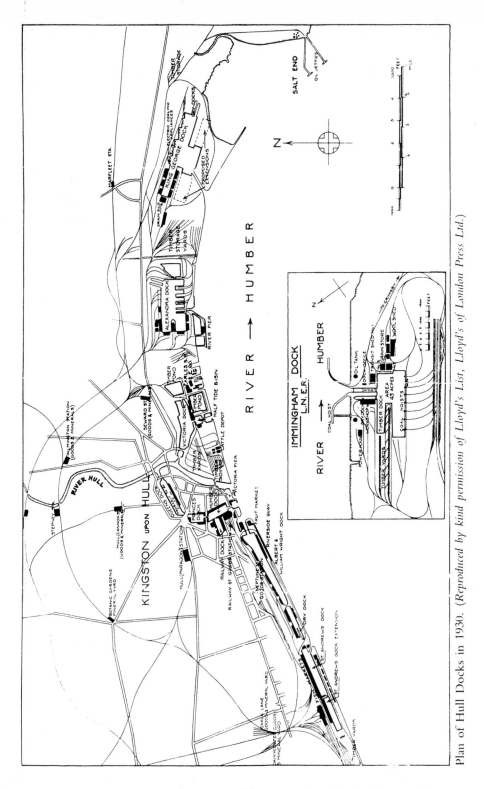

Plan of Hull Docks in 1930. *(Reproduced by kind permission of Lloyd's List, Lloyd's of London Press Ltd.)*

machine was stabled in a small shed at the station, accesss to which was through a wicket-gate beside the level crossing, unless, as quite often had happened, the crossing gates were partially opened to save me the awkward manoeuvre of leaning over the handlebars to unlock the wicket and hold it open against the spring. Each evening during the strike, there had been a little goup of men standing, silent and watchful by the crossing when I returned, and once as I leant forward to unlock the wicket, the signalman amongst them reached out his hand and took my key. Our eyes met, but no word was spoken as he unlocked the gate and held it open. He was Sam Watson, always, I think, the one with whom I was in closest rapport.

Hull Docks

While I was on my fortnight's holiday in the autumn of 1926, I learnt that I was to return, not to County Durham, but to Kingston-upon-Hull, to the office at King George Dock.

There was plenty to see in Hull, the third largest port in Britain, an ancient port with a long and distinguished history dating from 1293 when Edward I bought the site and founded the King's Town with quays along the west bank of the river Hull. Fierce storms and tides had destroyed two ports which had once flourished on the inner side of Spurn Head, and the creeks of a third, Hedon, had silted up, so there was need of a new port with sheltered berths on water scoured by the tides but not threatened by them.

The city grew rapidly, and, because there was excellent local clay but no building stone, brick was used in the fourteenth century for the splendid parish church and the protective walls with towers and gates. Before the end of the eighteenth century, the first floating harbour, Queen's Dock (1774), was built with brick walls. Humber Dock followed in 1806 and Prince's Dock in 1825, these three forming the chain of the Town Docks between the river Hull and the Humber, outside the line of the old city walls. Railway Dock, opening from Humber dock, was added in 1846. Thereafter, the docks spread westward along the waterfront: Albert Dock (1860), William Wright Dock (1866), St Andrew's Dock (by 1884); and eastward beyond Victoria Dock (1854) to Alexandra Dock (1885) and King George Dock (1914). By April 1922, all these docks, with an area of 220 acres and stretching for seven miles along the Humber waterfront, were owned by the North Eastern Railway. Owning others at Middlesbrough, Hartlepool, Wearmouth, Tyne Dock, and coal staithes at Blyth and Dunston-on-Tyne, the North Eastern was the largest dock owner in Britain. But although it had part share in some shipping, it owned none outright. Even the ferry service across the Humber from Hull Corporation's Victoria Pier to New Holland was maintained by paddle steamers belonging, not to the North Eastern but to the Great Central.

The Great Central also contributed substantially to the London & North

Humber Dock from the entrance lock. 23 October 1926.

Albert Dock, cold stores and warehouses. S.S. *Primo* of Newcastle alongside.

Albert Dock, ten-ton steam
travelling crane. 23 October
1926.

Victoria Corporation Pier, Great Central New Holland ferry alongside.

Eastern's maritime interests, owning the docks at Grimsby, which the company had greatly developed and from which their ships plied across the North Sea; and the fine Immingham Dock, six miles from Grimsby, constructed mainly for shipment of coal from South Yorkshire, which had been opened by King George V in 1912. Further south was the Great Eastern's very valuable contribution, the port of Harwich, from whose Parkeston Quay the company's prestigious Continental services sailed, also the docks at Felixstowe and the harbour at Lowestoft, the latter ranking after Grimsby and Hull as the third most important British fishing port. In Scotland, the North British was the largest dock owner: Methil and Burntisland engaged in shipment of coal from the Fife coalfield; Bo'ness further up the Firth of Forth; and the west coast port of Silloth on the Solway Firth, trading with the Isle of Man and importing Irish cattle. The North British also owned a number of ferry and river steamers, the chief of which were the Clyde paddle steamers plying from their pier at Craigendoran. Of the principal constituent companies, the Great Northern alone had no direct maritime interests; even the Great North of Scotland served fishing ports. But without any help from these two, the LNER became the greatest dock and harbour owner in Britain.

Besides fostering the existing ports and steamer services, the LNER introduced the first train–ferry service from British shores, by the Harwich–Zeebrugge route, begun in 1924 by a subsidiary company using three steamships built for the government during the 1914–18 war to carry equipment in railway wagons direct from factory to front line, plying between Richborough, near Sandwich in Kent, and the French port of Dunkirk.

Docks, and their shipping, have always drawn me to them, and I spent many hours at weekends walking around those at Hull. The two largest were Alexandra Dock and King George Dock. The former had been built by the Hull & Barnsley Company with valuable support from Hull Corporation, and when opened in the same month as the railway, July 1885, it was one of the largest and best equipped in the country, with cranes and hoists hydraulically worked. A riverside quay, where ships could lie alongside whatever the level of the tide, was added about 1907. This was rather hard on the North Eastern which then owned no docks at Hull. It had been prepared to buy out the Hull Dock Company in 1865 and modernise the equipment of the town Docks, but had been frustrated by the Dock Company's unwillingness to sell and by the opposition of the City corporation, as also was its proposal to construct a new deep water dock. However, a rate war between the Hull & Barnsley and the Dock Company, fuelled by a reduction of the North Eastern's charges for carriage of coal to the port, quickly brought the two former companies to the verge of collapse, and so in 1893 consent was at last obtained for the North Eastern to take over the Dock Company, on condition that during the next seven years it would

Alexandra Dock, 100-ton steam coaling crane. 24 October 1926.

King George Dock entrance lock; S.S. *Eros* of Helsingborg on the way out, towed by the tug *Merman*. 16 October 1926.

King George Dock. Electric cranes and, far right, coal hoists. 16 October 1926.

King George Dock. Two-storey ferro-concrete warehouses. 16 October 1926.

King George Dock. Numbers 6 and 7 hoists, showing low level sidings for laden wagons and high level viaduct for empties devoid of wagons during the mining dispute. 17 October 1926.

King George Dock. No 7 hoist, which was moveable, and high level gravity sidings for empty wagons. 17 October 1926.

spend half-a-million pounds on improvement. As for the plan to build a new dock, that was made contingent on the consent of the Hull & Barnsley Company. Six years later, this was secured by agreement that the two would share in its construction. Work on it was begun in 1906, but unexpected difficulties delayed completion, and it was June 1914 before it was ready for opening by King George V, who gave his name to it.

Like Alexandra Dock, the joint dock was equipped for the shipment of coal, but with electric hoists and cranes and a better arrangement of sidings, laden wagons running down a slight gradient to the foot of each hoist, empties being released on a high level viaduct along which they also ran by gravity. In October 1926, the sidings were almost empty because of the prolonged dispute in the mining industry, but although this was not officially over until the end of November, some miners had drifted back to work from August onwards, and as small supplies were reaching Hull, there was a strange sight of coal being simultaneously exported and imported.

The most animated scene at King George Dock was when an Elders & Fyffe ship tied up: banana vans, vacuum braked and steam heated, waited on the quayside to be despatched in express freight trains, and the transfer from ship to van was done entirely by manual labour, a queue of dockers standing ready to shoulder the hands of bananas as these were passed down from the ship.

Import of oil, though far from its present importance, was increasing, so the joint dock committee built an oil terminal at Salt End Jetty, to the east of the new dock. It was 1,500 feet long so that tankers could lie alongside at any

Alexandra Dock. Discharging imported coal from S.S. *Ellenborg* of Copenhagen. 5 October 1926.

94

King George Dock. Unloading bananas from Elder & Fyffes S.S. *Zent*.

Special trains for the bananas on the quayside. On the left are old North Eastern brake vans with 'birdcage' lookouts for the guard. 14 October 1926.

In mid-October, Edward Prince of Wales came to King George Dock while on an official visit to Hull, and from the dock office we watched him drive through the gates, looking very bored and unable to raise a smile even for the Wolf Cubs lining the roadside. 13 October 1926.

Albert Dock and the North Eastern Riverside Quay from the bridge of the Ellerman Line S.S. *Rollo*. 23 October 1926.

Riverside Quay, North Eastern Railway, no longer used for the passenger trains it was provided for. 23 October 1926.

Riverside Quay as depicted on a postcard issued by the company. The artist had evidently been instructed to show it as busy as the North Eastern hoped it would prove to be! The card gives its length as 2,500 feet, and states: 'Covered throughout. Station for passengers and emigrants. Steamers berth at any state of the tide. Fruit and other traffic loaded direct to truck.'

stage of the tide and discharge their cargo through pipelines to the storage tanks ashore.

To the west of the city, St Andrew's was the busy fish dock. William Wright and Albert Docks were in line and used by steamers of the Ellerman Wilson Line. Alongside Albert Dock, the North Eastern had built Riverside Quay in 1907, with a passenger station, as it was hoped to develop a passenger and cargo service to Zeebrugge, operated jointly with the Lancashire & Yorkshire Railway, using L&Y steamers. But in spite of a boat train with through coaches from Liverpool, Manchester, Glasgow and Newcastle, the service was never well patronised, and after the 1914–18 war, little but cargo was carried. So the station tracks became filled with wagons.

A Saturday afternoon spent among these western docks had an unexpectedly delightful ending. Having seen me busy with my camera, the chief officer of the Ellerman S.S. *Rollo* invited me aboard and took me to the bridge. Of course, that was a splendid viewpoint for a photograph, but that was not all, as he and the captain afterwards entertained me to tea in the captain's cabin.

Four years later, the LNER sold the old Queen's Dock to Hull Corporation. It was partly filled to form the sunken Queen's Gardens, opened in 1935. The other town Docks, outdated and no longer needed for trade, were also sold later to the Corporation. Victoria Dock has been filled in, Humber Dock is a marina, and at Prince's Dock, part of the water area is likely to be preserved, together with the handsome buildings facing the quays.

CHAPTER SIX

LONDON & NORTH EASTERN RAILWAY MAGAZINE

The first issue of the *London & North Eastern Railway Magazine*, in January 1927, was not Number One of Volume One, as might be expected, but Number One of Volume Seventeen. Both the North Eastern and the Great Eastern had started staff magazines in January 1911, so each had completed its sixteenth volume with the issue of December 1926. The scope of the former had been widened in July 1924 to cover Scotland, so that even before the initiation of the all-line periodical, the work of the editor, E.M. Bywell, had increased; and as he was also Curator of the Railway Museum Collection, he had to ask for assistance.

I had sent photographs and the occasional paragraph to the *North Eastern and Scottish Magazine*, which was, I suppose, why I was chosen to help him. Sorry though I was to leave Saltmarshe, I was elated by the thought of this new posting as I made my way to York by an awkward and time-consuming journey, which had to be repeated for several days until I found lodgings in the City.

Quite a number of the pre-1923 railway companies had encouraged production of a staff magazine, not only the more important ones such as the Great Western, London & North Western and London & South Western, but also the Furness which, with its feet in the Lake District, was well aware of the value of publicity, as also, of course, was the Great Central, whose Journal had been started by Sam Fay in 1905, but had ceased publication several years before the grouping.

Much space was occupied by staff news, such as individual postings, retirements, obituaries, social events including dinners, outings, lectures, debates and sporting activities; but there were also articles on leading personalities, railway operating methods, prestige trains, locomotive developments, large stations and depots, works of improvement, and resorts served; in addition, there were short paragraphs extracted from letters in a

News and Notes section. A magazine encouraged interest and keenness among the staff, but while it was intended primarily for them, there was much to appeal to outsiders interested in railways and copies were on sale at station bookstalls.

The LNER magazine had an editorial representative in the area general manager's office in London and Edinburgh, and a widespread chain of voluntary agents who acted as distributors and would also receive and forward contributions. In the first issue Bywell reported that 45,000 copies had been ordered, and within two months he received an encouraging letter from a former Great North of Scotland employee, who had gone to an American railroad nearly twenty years earlier but still liked to keep in touch, in which he claimed that the LNER magazine was far better produced and more interesting than those published by U.S.A. railroads.

On several occasions while I was with him, Bywell was offered articles for which the contributors wanted illustrations, so I had enjoyable days with my camera in their company; but, kind man that he was, he also arranged visits to other places in which I was particularly interested.

Testing a Sentinel-Cammell Steam Railcar

The first occasion on which I acted as 'official photographer' was during the testing of a new type of Sentinel-Cammell steam railcar. The inroads of road competition had long prompted the search for a vehicle which could operate a branch line more economically, and yet more frequently, than a loco-motive hauled train. Many railways had built steam railmotors, as the Great Western had in 1903, though no other had approached that company's total of a hundred cars. The North Eastern preferred the so-called autocar train, formed with an engine and one coach, or sandwiched between two coaches with end driving compartments. The company had also experimented with petrol engined cars, one of them a rail-mounted Leyland bus, and had built three superior petrol-electric coaches in 1903 which continued in service for twenty-eight years, but it was obviously preferable to use coal mined in the area rather than imported oil.

Aware of a possible new opening, the Sentinel Wagon Works, makers of successful (if dirty) steam road wagons, therefore collaborated with Cammell Laird & Co. in the production of railcars early in the 1920s, the first going into service on, I think, one of the Jersey railways in 1923. After experience with several early cars, the LNER played a leading part in their development, and eventually had a fleet of about seventy, in addition to eleven of a slightly different type designed by another firm which made steam road wagons, but these Clayton cars were less successful. The early Sentinel-Cammell vehicles, of which the LNER had twenty, were fitted with a two-cylinder engine, but while this was adequate for the vehicle alone on easily graded lines, it did not satisfy the traffic department, which

North Eastern steam autocar set, a push-pull set with end windows in the driving compartments of the two coaches, between which is No 465, one of Edward Fletcher's 0-4-4 BTP (Bogie Tank Passenger) engines of 1874–83. Passing Hylton, County Durham, on a Durham–Sunderland express service. 20 April 1926.

North Eastern Petrol-Electric Autocar, built 1903 for branch line service. Photograph by courtesy of the North York Moors Historical Railway Trust.

demanded enough power to haul a trailer when necessary, or even a horse box, up the steep gradients found on many branches.

The new car, No 22, had been designed to meet these conditions. It had a six-cylinder engine of 80hp, fed by a vertical boiler working at 250lb pressure, and was taken out on 6 April 1927 to test its ability to tow a horse box up the gradient of 1 in 43 from Whitby to Robin Hood's Bay on the coast line. The party of about twenty included representatives from Sentinel, Cammell Laird and the Yorkshire Post, the NE Area Passenger Manager (J.T. Naisby) and his Assistant (P.A. Harverson), L. Ballan, the Assistant to the Superintendent, and three others from his department concerned with traffic operation, the York District Superintendent, an inspector from the Locomotive Running Department – in fact, one or more from every section that would be concerned in the future; as well as a driver, fireman and guard, and the headquarters Porter (really a very delightful and efficient Commissionaire) to look after our well-being.

No more splendidly scenic route could have been chosen: from York to Malton, following the winding course of the river Derwent through the gap between the Howardian Hills and the Wolds, then northwards to Pickering and through Newton Dale by Goathland to Grosmont, a ride which I have always considered to be one of the most beautiful in England (abandoned by BR but now operated by the North York Moors Historical Railway Trust). The return from Whitby was by the coastal line through Robin Hood's Bay and Ravenscar to Scarborough, with splendid views of cliff and sea. It was a typical April day of showers and sunshine, the car was comfortable, there

Sentinel-Cammell Steam Railcar No 22, in LNER varnished teak livery, at Whitby Town, 6 April 1927. The car was later painted green and cream and named *Brilliant*.

At Robin Hood's Bay, detaching a horse box hauled up the gradient of 1 in 43 from Whitby as part of the test on 6 April 1927.

The official party in front of the car at Falsgrave, Scarborough. Seventh from the left is Engineer Commander Gaud from the Sentinel Wagon Works. L. Ballan, Assistant to the Superintendent, is the tall figure in the centre. The bearded figure fifth from the right is J.T. Naisby, North Eastern Area Passenger Manager; to the left of him, wearing a trilby hat, is Lieutenant Colonel Cockburn from Cammell Laird & Co, and behind him, wearing a bowler, P.A. Harverson, Assistant Passenger Manager.

were well-stocked hampers of food and drink, a maximum speed of 50 mph was attained, the horse box was successfully taken up the formidable gradient from Whitby to Robin Hood's Bay where it was detached, and it was a very friendly party that posed for me in front of the railcar at Falsgrave, Scarborough. Without doubt, it was a very pleasant day's outing for all of us. Nevertheless, the search for still more power continued, and twelve-cylinder cars were built subsequently.

No 22 had been finished in the dignified LNER teak, but, like the rest of the fleet, it was later painted green and cream, and in that colourful livery Sentinel-Cammell cars gave good service in many parts of the north-east for twenty years.

Northallerton's Milk Traffic

The North Eastern Railway had a large number of branch lines reaching out westwards from the York–Newcastle main line, penetrating Pennine dales of great beauty, tapping mineral resources, gathering farming produce, and providing passenger services to remote settlements. Three passed through the range: Newcastle–Carlisle by the Tyne and Irthing valleys; Darlington to Tebay and Penrith up Teesdale and over Stainmore to the Eden valley; Northallerton–Hawes following the River Ure up Wensleydale and over to Garsdale. This last, forty miles long, served a district yielding rich dairy produce, milk, cream, butter and cheese, which was brought down to Northallerton whence it was despatched to widespread destinations. The Northallerton stationmaster was preparing an article for the magazine, so towards the end of April I was sent off to provide the illustrations.

This was some six years before the introduction of six-wheeled tank wagons lined with glass or built of stainless steel, so all the milk then handled at Northallerton was in churns. Twenty-six six-wheeled milk vans, suitable, like the later tank wagons, for running in fast specials or attached to passenger trains, were allocated to the station and although every passenger train on the Wensleydale branch included one or more, milk specials were run several days a week. Some vans were despatched regularly to Newcastle, Hull, Scarborough, Hartlepool, and as far afield as Finsbury Park. Even so, almost every train calling at Northallerton station picked up full churns and set down empty ones.

The dairy farmers had established a co-operative, the Wensleydale Pure Milk society, which had built a dairy with a loading platform and sidings at Northallerton in 1905. Through it passed more than a million gallons a year, some set aside for making cream, butter and cheese, some filtered and Pasteurised for public sale. The Society owned a zinc-lined, ventilated van to collect churns from the branch stations, built for them by the North Eastern Railway in the ugly flat-sided style adopted for a short time in 1907.

Cream, about a thousand gallons a month, received special attention after

The Wensleydale Pure Milk Society's dairy at Northallerton. 26 April 1927.

Milk Special ready to leave Northallerton for the Hawes branch behind NE 0-6-1 No 611. 26 April 1927.

The Society's six-wheeled milk van. Standing in front is the Northallerton stationmaster, H.C.R. Calver.

The 'Cream Special' being pushed from the dairy to the station platform. Note the red flag, and the contact shoes between the wheels to operate the track circuits as the bogie crossed the main lines.

extraction at the dairy. Churns and cans for evening despatch by fast passenger trains had to be transferred to the station platforms, and for this they were loaded on a peculiar four-wheeled bogie, flying a red flag from a tall post and fitted with contact shoes to ensure operation of the track circuits as it was pushed by two men across the main lines – primitive, but effective!

Some London Goods Depots

In May I went to London to photograph some goods depots which the sub-editor at Liverpool Street suggested were worth recording. The visit also enabled me to see the next issue of the LNER Magazine rolling off the presses in the printing works of Harrison & Sons.

The large goods stations at the London termini were well enough known, so those to which I was taken were the Great Northern's City goods station at Farringdon Street and three obscure Great Eastern sites. Farringdon Street, reached via the Metropolitan Railway widened lines, was valuable as it avoided cartage through the busy streets from King's Cross. Wagons were dealt with on two levels; the lower entered direct from the sidings fanning out from the shunting neck to serve benches (timber goods platforms) and roadways below the warehouse; the upper, in the warehouse at street level, reached by means of hydraulic wagon hoists.

The first of the Great Eastern sites I was taken to was the East London Hoist on a spur viaduct between Bishopsgate goods station and Bethnal Green Junction. Taking two wagons, this 40-ton hoist lowered them to the East London Railway, over which the LNER ran goods trains for interchange with the Southern Railway at New Cross. These passed through the Thames Tunnel, the first beneath the river, driven between Wapping and Rotherhithe under great difficulties by the Brunels, father and son, between 1825 and 1843 and little used, except by pedestrians, until bought for the East London Railway in 1865. The other two sites were on Bow Creek, where the Great Eastern had goods stations at Canning Town and Blackwall, with wharves which were amongst the very few not owned by the Port of London Authority. Traffic was exchanged with barges working to and from the docks, and while eight of these lay on the mud alongside Canning Town wharf, wagons were being shunted by 0-4-0 tank No 7227, one of five powerful little locomotives built by the Great Eastern betweeen 1913 and 1921, specially designed by A.J. Hill with a very short wheelbase to negotiate the sharply curved tracks at these riverside depots.

The LNER in Manchester

Next there was a visit to Manchester, prompted by J.A. Jenkinson, the Assistant District Superintendent, who supplied notes to accompany my photographs in the November issue. The principal Great Central terminus consisted of three platforms and offices in the London Road terminus of the

Farringdon Street good station built by the Great Northern Railway on land leased from the Metropolitan Railway in 1873. 3 May 1927.

The East London Hoist, giving the Great Eastern access to the East London Railway. 3 May 1927.

The Great Eastern's goods station and wharf at Canning Town on Bow Creek.

0-4-0 shunting locomotive No 7227, still in Great Eastern wartime livery, at Canning Town, 3 May 1927.

The frontage of London Road station, Manchester, as rebuilt in 1866, showing the LNER portion on the left. 8 June 1927.

Liverpool to Harwich Continental express leaving Manchester Central station, headed by Great Central Director class 4-4-0 No 5438 *Worsley Taylor*. 8 June 1927.

It was preceded by a Midland train to Sheffield drawn by a class 3 4-4-0. In the sidings to the right are a Midland 0-6-4 tank and another GC 4-6-0.

Great Central 4-6-0 No 5424 *City of Lincoln* at the head of a train in Manchester Central station. 8 June 1927.

London & North Western, which had been rebuilt in 1866 and was later to be rebuilt again as Piccadilly station. But the GC was also one-third owner with the Great Northern and the Midland of the Cheshire Lines, and so had access to the joint committee's Central station, noted for its great single-span arched roof, similar to that at St Pancras and only thirty feet less. This was used by GCR through trains, such as the Liverpool–Harwich Continental express, which I photographed as it left. Alongside was the CLC goods station, and, beyond that, Deansgate goods, opened by the Great Northern Railway in 1898 when the approaching completion of the Great Central's London extension foreshadowed the end of the two companies' collaboration in working Manchester–London traffic. Great Northern goods trains reached it by exercising existing running powers over the GC from Nottingham.

The Great Northern certainly made its independent presence known in style. Ducie Street, the Great Central depot close to London Road station where GN goods had previously been handled, was very old fashioned: four tracks laid in stone setts for the draught horses which did the shunting, a warehouse on one side, sheds on the other, all entered by short sidings at right angles reached across little turntables for four-wheeled wagons. Deansgate, by contrast, was equipped with a huge five-storey warehouse boldly proclaiming its ownership in white lettering below the parapet. Built of brick, with steel beams supported by box-girder columns to carry brick-arched floors, it was said to have cost a million pounds and to be fireproof; it is an impressive monument to the railway age. Tracks entered

Ducie Street goods station, Manchester, a Great Central inheritance from the early days of the Manchester Sheffield & Lincolnshire Railway.

The Great Northern's Deansgate goods station in Manchester, built in 1898, showing the ramped viaducts leading to the two lower storeys of the great warehouse. 8 June 1927.

the two lower floors from high and low level sidings on ramped viaducts from the main yard.

The Great Central provided the locomotives to work the trains of the Cheshire Lines Committee, and also of the Manchester South Junction & Altrincham Railway which it owned jointly with the LNWR; and it was over this suburban line that Jenkinson took me to Brooklands for a very good lunch at a hotel he favoured.

The Electrified Mineral Line

As I mentioned in Chapter Three, when describing my first journey along the North Eastern main line, one of the signs of the company's enterprise which I was on the look out for was the electrified mineral line near Aycliffe. Since then, I had listened enthralled to one of the lectures in the course on Railway Operating which had dealt with that electrification, jotting down notes at the time and transcribing them later. I must have told Bywell of my interest, as, although no photographs were then needed for an article on a subject fully covered years earlier, he arranged for me to visit Shildon and ride down on one of the electric locomotives hauling a mineral train from there to Newport, near Middlesbrough.

Shildon marshalling yard was a gathering point for wagons from many collieries in the west of County Durham laden with coal destined for the iron

Brooklands station, Manchester South Junction & Altrincham Railway, as a train of MSJ&A coaches drawn by a GC 2-4-2 tank engine was arriving.

and steel works on Tees-side or the ports, to which they were distributed from the Erimus marshalling yard at Newport. Part of the route was historic: the original line of the Stockton & Darlington Railway from Shildon to Simpasture, thence the Clarence Railway as far as Carlton, opened in 1833. From there the route ran southwards and then eastwards through Thornaby towards Middlesbrough. The route mileage was fifteen, but with double track and yard lines, a total of 50 miles had to be equipped.

Designed by Vincent Raven, Chief Mechanical Engineer of the North Eastern, in collaboration with Charles Merz of Merz & McLellan, a well known firm of consultant electrical engineers, this was a very different matter from the North Tyneside suburban electrification of 1904. Whereas the motor coaches of the latter used direct current at 600 volts collected from a third rail, the mineral trains were to be hauled by Bo-Bo locomotives of 1,100hp drawing 1,500 volts DC from overhead wires. Ten of these, numbered 3 to 12 (following on the Tyne Quay pair of 1904), were built at Darlington with electrical equipment by Siemans.

Electric traction began in 1915, and down the grade from Shildon to Erimus the locomotives hauled trains of up to 1,400 tons at a maximum speed of 25 mph. The return journey included climbs of 1 in 104 for 1¾ miles and 1 in 230 for 4½ miles, over which an engine on test hauled an 800 ton train of ninety-two empty wagons. In spite of the high capital cost of the electrification, Raven claimed an economic success, five electric engines being able to do the work of thirteen steam ones for less than three-quarters of the cost per train-mile. Unfortunately, the later decline in the coal trade and north-eastern industries in general destroyed the advantage, and electric traction was abandoned as uneconomic in 1935.

114

North Eastern Railway electric locomotive No 10, 1100 hp, built at Darlington with electrical equipment supplied by Siemens, for the 1500 volt electrification brought into use on the Shildon–Newport mineral line in 1915.

Shildon locomotive shed on 30 June 1927. Six idle locomotives show the extent to which traffic had fallen off even then.

No 6, the locomotive on which I rode, ready to leave Middridge sidings, Shildon, for Newport with a train made up mostly with high-sided NE hopper wagons.

However, long before this happened, traffic between York and Newcastle had become so great that it was considered the capacity of the line would have to be increased. Moreover, the exigencies of wartime had left the North Eastern stock of steam locomotives depleted and run down, so, as an alternative to building 208 new ones and quadrupling the tracks at great expense, Raven proposed electrification, based on the experience already gained at Shildon. In October 1919, he and the superintendent (the officer responsible for traffic working) presented a report to the directors, claiming that 109 electric locomotives would be able to do the work of 209 steam ones with a great saving in operating costs. Raven was an able engineer, but a masterful man who well knew how to present an overwhelming mass of statistics, which, as everyone knows, can readily be used to prove a case. The directors were not fully convinced, but they gave him authority to build a prototype express locomotive, capable of hauling a 450 ton train of fourteen coaches at 65 mph on the level, and of reaching a maximum speed of 90 mph if necessary.

Built at Darlington with electrical equipment by Metropolitan-Vickers, No 13 appeared in May 1922, a graceful 2-Co-2 of 1,800hp with driving wheels 6 feet 8 inches in diameter as on an express steam locomotive. One of the problems with electric propulsion is whether the weight of the motors should be carried wholly or partly by the axles, or entirely by the fully sprung body of the vehicle, the former giving a simpler form of transmission

116

but causing heavier wear on the rails, the latter, in most cases at that date, transmitting the drive through cumbersome connecting and coupling rods. Raven disliked the idea of rods for a high speed locomotive and chose instead what is called 'quill-drive', a hollow shaft which surrounded the axle and was turned by the motor through gear wheels, itself transmitting the drive through strong helical springs to the spokes.

During a series of tests between Shildon and Newport, No 13 proved her ability to do all that was expected of her, on one occasion hauling twenty-two coaches (about 700 tons), on others working heavy trains of loaded or empty mineral wagons. As for speed, it seems certain that she exceeded 60 mph, but the claim that she reached 85 mph over tracks used only by mineral trains and maintained to a much lower standard than a main

Sir Vincent Raven's 2-Co-2 express locomotive, designed with the York–Newcastle electrification in mind. Built at Darlington with electrical equipment supplied by Metropolitan-Vickers in 1922. From a print in my collection.

line is open to doubt. However that may be, informed opinion states that in design and performance she was far ahead of her time.★

Unfortunately, the North Eastern was asked to delay implementation of the scheme while a government committee selected a uniform system for future electrification in Britain. This took them a year, and by 1921, when they concluded that one identical with that recommended by Merz & McLellan was the most suitable (as it continued to be considered for some thirty years), conditions were very different. The North Eastern main line was able to carry the traffic then flowing after the coal strike of 1921, and the

★ See *The Concise Encyclopaedia of World Railway Locomotives*: London, Hutchinson 1959. Chapter 3, 'Electric Motive Power' by F.J.G. Haut, B.Sc., A.M.Inst.Mech.Eng., page 156.

impending reorganisation of the railways made the Board of Directors understandably reluctant to embark on high capital expenditure. So the York–Newcastle electrification was laid aside, and the splendid No 13 languished at Darlington until she was at last sent to be scrapped in 1950.

A Visit to Scotland

Although I had never crossed the border and had no Scottish ancestry, Scotland had held a romantic fascination for me from early childhood: perhaps it derived from what I had read of the exciting triumphs of the railway builders, perhaps from the glamour of the Anglo–Scottish expresses described and pictured in magazines and books.

Bywell soon gave me an opportunity to go there, arranging for me to meet the Edinburgh sub-editor on a Monday morning in June and letting me catch the morning train from York the previous Saturday, so that I would be in Waverley station by 1.44 p.m. with a weekend ahead of me. As it turned out, I saw more of Scotland than I had dreamed possible, for there on Waverley platform, prominently displayed, was notice of a Sunday half-day excursion to Fort William. Obviously, the opportunity of travelling over the West Highland Railway for five shillings was one not to be missed.

The train was made up with nine corridor coaches, one North Eastern flat-sided vehicle amongst eight North British, one of which was a dining car, a useful provision on an excursion lasting twelve hours from start to

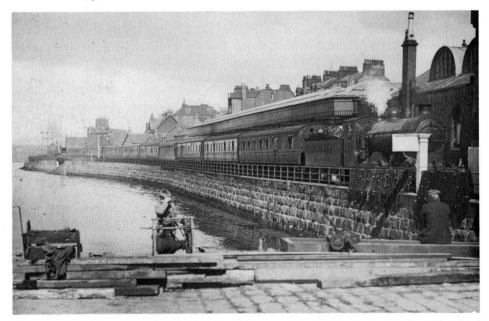

Excursion train from Edinburgh in Fort William station beside Loch Linnhe. The third vehicle is the heavy North British dining car, the fourth, the North Eastern coach built in the flat-sided style of 1907. 12 June 1927.

118

North British 4-4-0 No 9405 *Glen Spean* at Fort William locomotive shed, where the excursion had paused for her to be detached, so that the long train would all be in the platform.

Ready for return: 9405 *Glen Spean* heading 9258 *Glen Roy*.

finish. It was a remarkable coach, comfortable and easy riding, one of six massive all-steel cars weighing 46 to 50 tons each, built in 1920 and the first diners owned by the North British, apart from part-share in ECJS and M&NB cars.

Near enough for a half-day excursion, the train left Waverley at 11 a.m., and after a pause at Cowlairs on the edge of Glasgow, was hauled by a pair of NB Glen class 4-4-0 locomotives, designed by W.P. Reid and built in 1913 with superheaters and coupled wheels 6 feet in diameter, ideal for the stiff gradients and sharp curves of the West Highland line. Although I have travelled over the route since then, and driven to most parts of it by car, that first journey is unforgettable. Much of it was spent in the restaurant car, through whose wide windows I could enjoy to the full the magnificent views, and where, between meals, the table enabled me to write an ecstatic letter home.

The sun shone most of the day, so that landscape and seascape appeared at their best, unlike a subsequent journey when all was shrouded in the mist and drizzle so common in the west. And what great variety of scenery there was to be enjoyed as I dashed wildly from one side to the other of the restaurant car! Gare Loch and Loch Long, the two sea lochs, were spread out below as the train climbed towards the pass from which Loch Lomond burst into sight. There were the forested beauty of Glen Falloch seen from the shelf and viaduct traversed by the railway; the ascent from Crianlarich through Strathfillan and Tyndrum; the famous horseshoe curve between Beinn Odher and Beinn Dorain, adopted to avoid building an expensive viaduct; Bridge of Orchy and Loch Tulla, and the long climb beside the Water of Tulla before emerging on Rannoch Moor.

From Rannoch station, a train from the south appeared over the horizon at the far end of the moor, more than five miles away across a sodden land seamed with water courses and speckled with lochans. No wonder the moor greedily swallowed earth tipped to form the track bed; no wonder a nine-span viaduct had to be built immediately north of Rannoch station where no bank would rise above a bog; no wonder the making of the line greatly exceeded the estimates. In the late summer of 1893, there was danger of the work coming to a standstill, until J.H. Renton, one of the directors, pledged his personal wealth to tide over a financial crisis. Grateful navvies later carried a huge boulder to the station, set it up on the platform and, using only their railway-building implements, carved Renton's head and shoulders.

A mile-and-a-half from Rannoch, where the railway passed through a rock cutting at a height of 1100 feet, a snow-shed had to be built, and fences of close-packed sleepers erected on the mountain side to stop drifting snow, because blizzards had closed the line here for weeks during the fierce winter of 1894-95, the very first after the line was opened. Further on, the summit was reached near Corrour, 1347 feet, and the descent began, passing Loch

Rannoch station, West Highland Railway, opened 1874. 23 July 1969.

Rannoch Moor, nine-span viaduct across a bog which had proved impossible to fill.
23 July 1969.

Rannoch station. Head and shoulders of J.H. Renton, the director whose wealth overcame a financial crisis, as carved by grateful navvies.

North British 4-4-0 No 9338 *Helen MacGregor* approaching Waverley station through Prince's Street Gardens, 11 June 1927. Engines of the Scot class, designed by W.P. Reid for express work, were built in 1909 and 1914.

Treig and going down Glen Spean, where the water, not then abstracted for a power station, cascaded over the Spean's rocky bed beside the track. And so to the finish beside Loch Linnhe, a hundred miles from Craigendoran where the West Highland line branched off the North British some twenty miles north-west of Glasgow.

I saw something of the City of Edinburgh on the Saturday afternoon, and in the evening, after dinner, caught a bus to South Queensferry for a sight of that engineering wonder, the Forth Bridge. Better still, I was able to walk across it on the Monday after meeting the sub-editor and securing a permit from the Engineer's Department. There was not the usual gale blowing up the Firth, so that, although drizzle threatened, the walk each way was enjoyable as well as fascinating.

Long before that memorable weekend was over, the 'romantic fascination' had become an incurable disease, only to be alleviated by visits from time to time and five happy years living in the centre of Scotland prior to retirement.

Entering the south cantilever of the Forth Bridge, No 9035 *Glen Gloy*.

North British 4-4-2 tank No 9039 in the centre of the south cantilever, bound for Edinburgh. 13 June 1927.

CHAPTER SEVEN

ROAD COMPETITION

After six blissful and very interesting months working with E.M. Bywell in his spacious and well equipped office on the first floor of the York headquarters, I was moved upstairs to the Area Passenger Manager's office, to a section combating road competition. I took over from one Traffic Apprentice, a university graduate of an academic cast of mind, and after six months was followed by another, a member of the clerical staff who had been selected after passing the Traffic Apprentices' examination that I had yet to sit. My successor, of whom I saw much during the next two years, became a personal friend.

Under the passenger manager's chief clerk, each of us in turn acted as secretary to a committee, presided over by P.A. Harverson, the Assistant Passenger Manager, appointed to counter the competition of local bus services; and as the Sentinel-Cammell cars became available, the committee put forward recommendations for increasing services and reducing fares on selected branch lines. The major problem was that our competitors, some of them sizeable firms but many of them small-scale operators with low overheads, could set and adjust their fares as they wished, free of the necessity to grade them according to distance in the way the railway company was.

Our personal duty was to collate information, record the decisions, and prepare the minutes of each meeting for circulation to the various departments involved. There was lively debate in committee, but the meetings were pleasant, and as some members had come from afar to attend them, we all lunched together at the Royal Station Hotel. As is the way with such deliberations, it took time to formulate proposals, more time to win approval, and yet more time to implement them, but the increased number of passengers carried over those branches dealt with was sufficiently encouraging for the experiment to be gradually extended.

Then, in the late summer of 1928, there came a directive from King's

Cross to reduce fares and improve train services as rapidly as possible over all branch lines where success appeared likely. By that time I had been posted to Ripon goods office, but I was recalled to York for several weeks to help my successor, and the preparation of proposals was entrusted to a group of about half-a-dozen of us, almost all of much the same age. There was pleasant companionship, and, provided with the time-tables and lists of fares of the bus operators, we worked hard, often late into the evening after feeding at the company's expense in the station restaurant. Some branches could be dealt with quickly on a systematic basis, but many proved extremely difficult, none more so than the York–Scarborough line running from the City in a great arc north-eastwards and then eastwards to reach the Derwent valley before following the twisting course of that river, whereas bus services followed shorter routes radiating from York like the spokes of a wheel. Try as we would, it was impossible to match the bus fares of independent owners when these were lower to a more distant point on the railway than to a nearer one. An unsatisfactory compromise was the only solution. One of our group, however, was a cock-sure ex-public school boy, and the rest of us so wearied of his criticism of our cautious progress that we gave him one particularly awkward line to deal with, telling him to get on with it on his own. This he did, and after we had gleefully shown up his inconsistencies, we had little further trouble with him!

Previous to this, however, and while I was still working in the passenger manager's office in York, an unexpected development in road transport had been brought to our notice. At that date, very few road passenger services covered long distances, but an advertisement had recently appeared in a Newcastle paper announcing an excursion by road to London for the autumn motor show of 1927. We at once began making enquiries, and these revealed that a similar excursion had been run the previous May, that during the summer months a regular service had developed leaving Newcastle three days a week, and that even as we collated information, a daily service had come into operation.

Up to this time, most railwaymen had seen road competition as a threat to short haul traffic only, and older members of the staff pooh-poohed the idea of anyone making a 274-mile journey by road when it could be made in half the time by train. In their opinion, all that the Newcastle–London vehicles could be doing was to pick up and set down short stage passengers en route. I had good reason to doubt this.

My home town of Cheltenham is 97 miles from London by road, but 121 miles by rail via Gloucester and Stroud over a route on which speeds were low until Swindon was passed. It was an ideal setting for road to compete with rail, and I knew very well that the Black & White Motor Company operated a well-established and well-patronised service between Cheltenham and London, using no mere country service vehicles, but (for those days) fast and comfortable coaches, and charging fares very much lower than the railway. The unwelcome competition had stung the Great Western into introducing a new and faster train in each direction. I therefore felt pretty certain that, although the Newcastle–London road service took twelve or thirteen hours, it was carrying a large proportion of long distance passengers attracted by the lower fares: £1 single, £1 10s. or £1 15s. shillings return, with the railway fare of £1 13s. 11d. single and £3 2s. 3d. or £3 17s. 10d. return.

I pressed the point, and in November 1927 the Passenger Manager authorised me to make a return journey. This proved what I had suspected, for almost all the passengers starting from Newcastle or picked up by the wayside in County Durham travelled either to London or to towns in the northern home counties. This news was sufficiently alarming for my report (of which I still have a copy) to be forwarded to the Chief General Manager; I expected it to go forward in the usual way, anonymously, but before sending it, the Passenger Manager, J.T. Naisby, a kindly man, bearded Edwardian fashion, called me into his office and bade me sign it. The result was a request from Sir Ralph Wedgwood for more information, and this set several of us on the roads in the pleasant month of May 1928.

By this time there were two services in each direction daily, Sunday included. The two principal operators were Orange Brothers of Bedlington, Northumberland, and R. Armstrong & Sons of Ebchester, County Durham; and as the latter's 'Majestic' service had the reputation of being the best managed and most reliable, I booked a seat on it and, after staying overnight in Newcastle, made my way to the Old Cattle Market at 7.30 a.m.

I took a notebook which I used as surreptitiously as possible, yet not without arousing some suspicion, and also my camera, which could not be concealed but which, as the pictures show, met with general approval. The journey proved unexpectedly eventful as well as revealing.

'At about 8 a.m.', I wrote in my report, 'a fine vehicle with large destination boards on the roof-sides appeared, and into this the seventeen waiting passengers mounted. It was a most comfortable vehicle, a twenty-six seater built by W. & G. du Cros of Acton, with well-upholstered and well-sprung seats, parcel racks, kitchen, lavatory, and roof-rack for luggage; there was plenty of space, and a comfortable journey seemed assured.'

Alas for our expectations! The two-man crew who had driven the du Cros in from Ebchester were not satisfied with its performance. Presently a much smaller vehicle arrived, a Reo, to which we transferred. It had less accommodating seats, restricted space, no racks for coats or cases – in fact, it was just a typical country bus, though the Reo marque had a reputation for speed. At 8.20 we were off. The Orange vehicles had got away long before us, but a splendid coach still languished at the starting point with only one passenger aboard. I had sampled this coach a few months earlier; it had been an outstanding exhibit at the previous motor show, and had been acquired by yet another Newcastle operator, one Glenton Friars. With a kitchen and

Newcastle-upon-Tyne, 8 May 1928. Waiting to board the du Cros coach intended for the Majestic service to London.

Cattrerick: 'What's wrong with the Reo?' The inferior vehicle substituted for the du Cros was not fit for the road either.

lavatory opposite one another, a narrow gangway between them led from the main passenger compartment to a rear 'Observation Lounge'. All the seats were very comfortable, but the vaunted culinary side was so limited that the crew preferred to stop even to boil a kettle for tea. The standard of signposting then prevailing along the Great North Road can be gauged by the fact that, after the tea stop, the driver of the Glenton Friars coach had lost his way in the gathering February darkness.

But to return to May and the Reo. Having crossed the Tyne into Gateshead, we saw two passengers waiting by the kerb, but there was no way of telling by which of the three services they had booked, and when we stopped, we learnt that they were waiting for the Glenton Friars coach. A little further on, at Low Fell, there was another passenger waiting, so again we stopped, and grateful he was, for although he had booked with Orange Brothers, he had been left stranded by their speeding buses; nevertheless, he had to pay his fare over again and apply to the rival firm for a refund.

However, if co-operation was lacking over bookings, we soon found that it was fully and readily given in emergency. The Reo engine was far from being in condition for the long run. New big ends had been fitted and the engine re-assembled only the previous evening. There was insufficient oil. So far from being able to show her paces, her speed was severely restricted, and presently the splendid Glenton Friars coach overtook us. Nevertheless, this nursing of the engine over the long straight stretches to Catterick Bridge was of no avail, for presently an ominous knocking resounded. Beside the racecourse, a brief stop was made and the engine inspected. The driver's fears were sufficiently allayed for us to set off again, but in less than a mile the unhealthy knocking sounded again and was quickly followed by an almighty crash. The vehicle came to a standstill. Clearly, further progress was impossible.

Fortunately the end had come exactly opposite Catterick Post Office, so one of the crew nipped across the road, telephoned Boroughbridge, twenty-one miles ahead, and succeeded in contacting the driver of one of the Orange buses just as he was about to leave, persuading him to return to pick us up. His vehicle was lightly loaded, but, as we learnt later, in order to make room for us, four of his passengers bound for Doncaster were transferred to another, probably the Glenton Friars.

So we sat disconsolately in the immobile Reo, expecting a wait of some forty-five minutes before the Orange bus could arrive to rescue us. Presently, however, a large Thorneycroft came in sight, slowed down and stopped for the driver to ask what ailed us. He was running on a Newcastle–Liverpool service and, as he had only three passengers aboard, he suggested carrying us forward until we should meet the returning Orange bus. So into the Thorneycroft the twenty of us piled with our baggage to ride for some fifteen miles to where the road to Ripon and Leeds diverged from the Great North road. There we transferred yet again, into a Gilford

Near Melmerby: transferring from the Thorneycroft, running the Newcastle–Liverpool service, to Orange Brothers' Gilford.

coach of Orange Brothers, the fourth vehicle in which we had sat on this eventful journey. It as not a particularly comfortable vehicle, no better indeed than many a country bus and certainly inferior to a Guy coach in which I had ridden from Withernsea to Hull nearly two years earlier.

Although no schedules were then published, it was obvious that we must be running very late, and the crew set out to make full use of the Gilford's power. 'There was some very fast running' states my report, and I noted in support (it reads strangely in these days) that several miles were covered at speeds of 31 to 40 mph and that 'very much higher maximum speeds occurred' – in fact, we topped the fifty once or twice, which was not bad in 1928 when the legal limit for passenger service vehicles was 20 mph. Of course the police had their eyes on these services, and although A.A. Scouts and other road users did their best to signal warnings, Orange Brothers had already been fined a considerable sum.

The remainder of the journey was uneventful. We stopped fifty-five minutes in Doncaster for lunch, and twenty minutes at a café beside the aerodrome at Wittering for tea, picked up a London-bound passenger at Biggleswade, set down at Stevenage, Welwyn, Tally-Ho Corner and Highgate before coming to a stand outside King's Cross station at 8.23 p.m.

Alas for the Majestic's reputation for reliability! When I joined Orange Brothers for the return journey next day, I was told that my up run was by

A pause on the way north on 9 May 1928: Orange Brothers' six-cylinder, 37hp Gilford, costing £1,200.

no means the only occasion when a Majestic vehicle had broken down, that their reputation had been destroyed utterly, and – unkindest cut of all – that Orange Brothers had refused to lend a vehicle for the northbound service unless the hiring charge of £20 was paid in advance.

We left King's Cross at 8 a.m. with seventeen passengers, but heavy early morning traffic heading for London made progress very slow until past Barnet. Thereafter, time was regained by driving at 45 to 50 mph, but this I had to estimate because the speedometer gave no reading – probably it had been disconnected to frustrate nosey passengers like myself! A rumour that between Biggleswade and Buckden the police were on the alert, led to such cautious driving that second gear had to be engaged for a time.

On we went, through the narrow street of Buckden and the wide market at Stilton, round the twisting junctions at delightful Wansford and across the River Nene by the single-track bridge, through the tortuous heart of graceful Stamford, over a level-crossing where the needs of the Great North road and the Great Northern Railway conflicted, stopping at Grantham for lunch in company with all the other Newcastle-bound coaches, and at Boroughbridge where 'tea was splendidly served at one of the hotels'. So into Newcastle at 7.45 p.m., the average speed, excluding stops, being just over 28 mph.

One passenger complained of the jolting and noise, and assured me that he would certainly have travelled by train had he anticipated the discomfort. But this was not the opinion of the majority. The weather had been kind, and they had enjoyed the continually changing backdrop of urban architecture and countryside, viewed so much more intimately than was possible from a train; or, indeed, is possible at all in our own day, as we speed along the by-passes and ribbons of dual-carriageway.

131

It had been a wholly uneventful journey, devoid even of the excitement of a near-miss such as had been experienced by a contemporary newspaper correspondent riding the Newcastle road. It was long before the days of 'Major Road Ahead', 'Give Way', or 'Stop' signs, and a van incautiously turned into the Great North Road in the path of the northbound coach. Each blew a horn obligato. Both accelerated in an attempt to draw clear. Collision was averted by a whisker, but the van overturned into the ditch. No one was hurt, so after a brief halt, the coach was quickly on its way again.

As well as the Newcastle–London services, others were examined. There was one from Middlesbrough to London, another from Newcastle to Edinburgh which proved to be a country bus stopping frequently to pick up and set down, and a reasonably fast service between Glasgow and Newcastle via Carlisle, on which I travelled in a very ordinary and not particularly comfortable vehicle which could not possibly be called a 'coach'. In fact, of all the vehicles I saw operating these long distance services, only Glenton Friars's and the du Cros justified use of that term.

CHAPTER EIGHT

THE WISBECH & UPWELL TRAMWAY

In the latter part of the nineteenth century and the early part of the twentieth, when horse-drawn vehicles were still the only means of rural transport, there was need of a cheap way of extending railways into areas where a normal branch line would not be economic. The Tramways Act of 1870 enabled a local authority, or a company, to obtain from the Board of Trade a provisional Order, subject to confirmation by Parliament, to lay a track along a public highway; but although these powers were normally used for laying street tramways with grooved rails, they could also sanction the formation of a line with edge rails laid along the verge of a roadway.

The Light Railways Act of 1896 went a step further, by empowering the Board of Trade (and its later offshoot, the Ministry of Transport) to authorise a new railway by promulgating an Order. This enabled promoters to avoid altogether the expense of a private Act, and also exempted the proposed line from most of the arduous regulations imposed by nineteenth-century railway legislation. Speed, however, was severely restricted, perhaps to a maximum of 25 mph, with a reduction to 10 mph at ungated level crossings.

What advantage was taken of these relaxations varied considerably from line to line, but the LNER and the other three groups all operated some light railways, often taken over from a small independent company which had promoted it. In the North Eastern Area, for example, there was the branch opened in 1898 by the Cawood Wistow & Selby Light Railway, which was taken over by the North Eastern in 1900 and long served by one of its petrol-electric railcars, or latterly by a Sentinel-Cammell steam car. Yorkshire also had a number of small independent railways, many of which I visited with keen interest and enjoyment. Some were standard gauge, others narrow, a few belonged to public utilities. Most had been built under the Light Railways Act, but some had obtained a private Act of Parliament.

Further away, in the eastern counties, on the Cambridgeshire-Norfolk border, the LNER operated one of the most intriguing branch lines in Britain: the Wisbech & Upwell Tramway. Although there were other steam tramways, this was the most purposeful and busiest; it was also the last to survive. It had been built by the Great Eastern Railway, and opened in August 1883 to serve the villages of Elm, Emneth, Outwell and Upwell, 5¾ miles from Wisbech station; and, authorised under the Tramways Act of 1870, it was laid almost entirely alongside public roads. There were five depots which handled goods and passengers, and twelve roadside sites at which passenger trams would stop by request. Freight traffic was considerable, for, serving part of the fertile Fenland, the tramway carried the agricultural produce of prosperous farms, and, in the soft fruit season, a rich crop of strawberries.

It was subject to special regulations. The locomotives were all built by the Great Eastern at Stratford Works with elaborate cladding to avoid scaring passing horses. 'The machinery', stated the regulations, 'shall be concealed from view at all points above four inches from the level of the rails, and all fire . . . shall be concealed from view.' So wheels and motion were hidden behind metal plates, and the boiler encased in a wooden body. Even a whistle was banned, and instead, warning of approach was given by a bell. Indeed, the only overt indication that it was a locomotive came from the thin plume of smoke rising from a diminutive stove-pipe chimney protruding through the roof and topped by a spark-arresting mesh. Front and back, there was a 'suitable fender to push aside obstructions' – evidently the term 'cow-catcher' was not recognised officially! Speed was restricted to 8 mph, so a speed-indicator was fitted, and a governor which would shut off steam and apply the brake if the driver let the rate rise to 10 mph. The first three were 0-4-0s with inside cylinders, designed by T.W. Wordsell, who later moved from the Great Eastern to the North Eastern. His successor, James Holden, added another five, before building ten more powerful ones to cope with increasing freight traffic: a six-coupled version with outside cylinders. To later generations, these delightful little locomotives became widely known from the Revd Awdry's story of *Toby the Tram Engine*.

Goods traffic was carried in ordinary open wagons and covered vans, except for the valuable strawberry crop which was loaded in ventilated fruit vans. At the height of the soft fruit season, a travelling office was attached, so that clerks set down at each depot on the outward journey to invoice the traffic could complete their work on the way back to Wisbech.

Passenger cars were built with floors much lower than usual, and a balcony at each end with steps for easy access from the road, for there were no platforms except at Wisbech station, where the rails used by the trams had therefore to be laid on a raised bed of ballast. Seats in the cars were against the sides, as in the street tramcar, so that the conductor-guard could pass along to issue tickets. Six of them were four-wheeled, but two larger ones built in 1890 were carried on bogies, and it was one of these that became

Wisbech station. No 7132 stands ready to leave for Upwell as Great Eastern Claud Hamilton 4-4-0 No 8896 runs in with a train for King's Lynn. The raised track bed beside the outer platform is very noticeable. 31 December 1927.

famous after withdrawal when it was equipped with a well stocked bar and used in 1952 for the comedy film, *The Titfield Thunderbolt.*

There were eight trips each way on Saturdays between 7.30 a.m. and 10.24 p.m., one less on other weekdays, but none on Sundays, and to allow for calls at the depots, the conditional halts, and mandatory stops approaching four highway crossings, the scheduled time for the journey of 5¾ miles was 39 minutes.

Of course, by the 1920s most people used the far quicker motor buses, so it was not surprising to learn that the passenger service would be withdrawn after 31 December 1927. I had long been familiar with pictures of the trams from postcards sent by my father when staying in the neighbourhood; but as I had never seen it, and that last day was a Saturday, I asked leave of absence and set out to reach Wisbech in time to take photographs during the morning before the December light should begin to fade. It meant an early start from York, about 3.30 a.m., by one of the night trains from Scotland. It was a morning so cold that, when I changed at Peterborough, I saw a coach with one end sheeted in ice from the roof downwards – water from the over-flow as a locomotive picked up from the track-troughs having frozen as it fell.

There was no need to hurry, as I had arranged to spend the weekend with my friends in Cambridge, so I had a leisurely breakfast at the Rose and Crown in Wisbech before boarding the 9.30 a.m. tram at the station. Clearly, the best plan was to ride to the terminus at Upwell and walk much of the way back, stopping here and there to take lineside photographs.

Upwell passenger station, with tram ready to leave for Wisbech behind 0-4-0 No 7133 of Great Eastern class G 15. The goods yard is to the left of the waiting room. 31 December 1927.

Upwell goods yard, showing plenty of evidence of flourishing freight traffic. 31 December 1927.

A picturesque scene in Outwell village, from a card postmarked August 1910. Horse-drawn vehicles were then the only competitors.

Tram to Upwell climbing the 1 in 30 gradient from Outwell Basin Depot to the bridge across the Wisbech Canal. 31 December 1927.

Boyce's Bridge. Goods tram from Wisbech in the loop, private owner wagons leading behind 0-4-0 No 7133. 31 December 1927.

Boyce's Bridge. 11.25 a.m. goods tram from Wisbech entering the loop to pass the 11.40 a.m. passenger tram from Upwell. 0-4-0 locomotives 07126 (left) and 7132 (right). 31 December 1927.

The 12.40 from Wisbech crossing New Common Bridge over the canal. 31 December 1927.

Elm Road Crossing. Passengers leaving the tram to walk into Wisbech, about 1920. The horse box in rear may have been carrying cattle. From an old postcard.

Upwell, approached over one of the few sections of reserved track, was the most important of the five depots, equipped with a brick waiting room, a goods office and half a dozen long sidings. At the others, there were a loop, sidings, office, and a shed for waiting passengers, all beside the road. Between the two depots at Outwell Village and Outwell Basin, there was the only sharp rise on the route, 1 in 30 to the bridge over the Wisbech Canal, one which, although short, was enough to be awkward for an engine with a heavy freight train.

Boyce's Bridge, about midway, was the only depot where trams were allowed to cross, and as there were no signals beyond the limit controlled by the main line signal box at Wisbech, safety depended upon strict adherence to the timetable, and on the man in charge who locked and unlocked the points when two were scheduled to meet. Here I was able to photograph one goods as it passed on its way to Upwell, and then a second, the 11.25 from Wisbech, as it entered the loop to cross the 11.40 passenger tram from Upwell. This I rode in as far as Elm Road Crossing, where the rails quitted the roadside for the reserved track leading to the junction. Old photographs show that Elm Road was the favourite alighting point, passengers finding it more convenient to walk into the town from there than from the station. I took one more photograph at New Common Bridge, only a few hundred yards away, but there had never been the sunshine I had hoped for, and the pale December light, though eked out by reflection from the snow-covered ground, was barely enough for pictures of even these slow-moving trams.

As I walked into the town, I felt that it had been well worth making the effort to see this quite exceptional feature of the LNER. However, although

Elm Road Crossing. G 15 0-4-0 No 0125 with fruit vans and passenger cars, posed with the road-sweeper! From an old postcard.

that day was the end of passenger carrying, freight working was maintained until May 1966, not indeed by the little steam tram engines, for those had been supplanted by diesels in 1952. Before catching the afternoon train to Cambridge, I made my way to the Rose and Crown again, where luncheon was a 'Farmers' Ordinary', a substantial three-course meal guaranteed to fill empty stomachs after a morning at the market (or walking beside the tramway!).

The York office kept New Year's Day as a holiday, so it was Monday evening when I returned, but as the Great Eastern Railway's through service had been discontinued by the LNER, by far the easiest way was via London. I caught the 7.20 from King's Cross, a train I used many times, which included sleeping cars for Fort William, Inverness via Forres as well as via Carr Bridge, Aberdeen, and, in the summer season, for Lossiemouth, the latter serving all the principal stations on the Great North of Scotland main line from Aberdeen. As far as York, the train had a dining car, a very comfortable twelve-wheeled, clerestory-roofed Great Northern vehicle of about 1900, excellently managed and serving the best dinners I have ever eaten on any train: four courses, after which a basket of fruit was handed round, all for five shillings and the price of beer and coffee.

CHAPTER NINE

YORK

The London & North Eastern's Railway Museum

While I was with E.M. Bywell in 1927, I saw much of the Railway Museum, of which he was Curator. It was not then open to the public, that came in 1928, but individual visitors and parties who applied were always shown round. It was my pleasure one day to accompany Cecil J. Allen, whose articles in the *Railway Magazine* and elsewhere had made him a boyhood idol. A party of German railway students came in May 1927, and that same month Bywell wrote in the LNER magazine of 'an ever-increasing stream' of visitors who had come by appointment.

The museum had been formed by the North Eastern Railway in 1922, partly to house some of the smaller exhibits intended for display at Darlington during the 1925 Railway Centenary Exhibition. Many of these had been collected by J.B. Harper, assistant superintendent, who, having had the formation of a museum in mind for some forty years, had been able to save many interesting relics from destruction. More items had come in response to a notice in the NER magazine asking members of the staff to report any objects they felt were worth preserving. Once it was known that a museum had been established, gifts came from private individuals, societies and public companies, from other constituents of the LNER, and even other railway companies, for there was no other railway museum in Britain. The Lambton Hetton & Joicey Collieries presented George Stephenson's Hetton Colliery locomotive, built in 1822, which they had preserved after withdrawing it from service in 1908; and in 1926, the Southern Railway gave an open third class carriage from the Bodmin & Wadebridge Railway.

The small items were housed temporarily in a basement room at the NER headquarters. Locomotives, rolling stock and other large exhibits were kept in a building alongside Queen Street, south of the station, which had been the machine shop of the locomotive repair works established by the York &

Patrick Stirling's 4-2-2 No 1, built for the Great Northern Railway in 1870, alongside Gresley Pacific No 2579 *Dick Turpin*, in York old station on 23 March 1927 before taking her place in the LNER Queen Street museum.

The Queen Street museum in 1927: Hetton Colliery locomotive of 1822 and LBSCR 0-4-2 *Gladstone*.

North Midland Railway in 1842. But as long as venerable and famous engines continued to be sent to this home for the aged, tracks had to remain on a bare concrete floor, and it was impossible to make any tidy arrangement.

The year 1927 was a particularly fruitful one. On 23 March, Patrick Stirling's Great Northern 4-2-2 No 1, with single driving wheels 8 feet 1 inch in diameter, came under her own steam from Doncaster, and was photographed alongside Gresley's Pacific *Dick Turpin* before going into the museum. Then, on 31 May, William Stroudley's LBSCR 0-4-2 *Gladstone* of 1882 arrived, on loan from the Stephenson Locomotive Society who had restored her after acquiring her from the Southern Railway. Another gift received the same day was a valuable collection which joined the small exhibits.

Of course, several North Eastern locomotives were there, the LNER having had the foresight to preserve two veterans which had appeared in the 1925 procession. 0-6-0 No 1275, built in 1874, was a Stephenson long boiler engine of a class which had been designed ten years earlier by William Bouch, Locomotive Superintendent of the Stockton & Darlington Railway; remarkable though it now seems, she depended for braking power entirely on the large wooden brake-blocks fitted to the tender. No 901 was a 2-4-0 express engine built by the NER at Gateshead in 1875 to Edward Fletcher's designs, a very handsome exhibit with open-work splashers, polished brasswork, and elaborate painting and lining. These two were joined in 1928 by the Tennant class 2-4-0 No 1463, built in 1885 and withdrawn in 1927.

By the summer of 1928, there had been a general tidying up at Queen Street. The building had been repaired and repainted, and locomotives and vehicles each stood upon a short length of track embedded in neat gravelled plots within boarded edges. Moreover, the small exhibits had been moved from their temporary quarters to what had been the first class refreshment room in York's original station. So when it was announced that there would be an exhibition of modern engines and rolling stock in York station on Sunday 17 June, the handbills advertising cheap tickets from Richmond, most stations south of Darlington, and all stations from Harrogate via Ripon, Melmerby and Thirsk, contained the first announcement that the museum was open to the public.* A great many visitors attended: more than 20,000 to see the exhibition in the station, 17,600 to Queen Street, and 10,700 to the display in the old refreshment room.

In 1931, the Great Western's famous *City of Truro* arrived (a sprightly old dame who has never fully accepted retirement!), and later came the diminutive Grand Junction 2-2-2 *Columbine* from the LMS, two Great Northern Atlantics, the NE 4-4-0 No 1621 of class M which took part in the record run during the race to Aberdeen in 1895; and 'The Pet', the 2-2-4

---

* This I recorded in a note made at the time.

144

North Eastern locomotives: 0-6-0 No 1275 built in 1874 to the designs of William Bouch, Locomotive Superintendent of the Stockton & Darlington, and 2-4-0 No 901 designed by Edward Fletcher and built in 1875.

Queen Street tidied up: Bodmin & Wadebridge Railway third class carriage, probably late 1830s, on track embedded in a gravel plot within boarded edges.

145

Aerolite, which, like other similar small tank engines, had long remained in use hauling official inspection saloons, *Aerolite* herself until 1933.

Here, then, in Queen Street, was a fine nucleus round which gathered later the splendid collection now in the National Railway Museum, housed in what was formerly York North locomotive shed. But displayed in the LNER museum were items of historical interest which are less easily seen now: some of them showed the development of the permanent way – tram-plates of 1775, cast iron fish-bellied edge rails of about 1825, pointwork of 1834, and bull-headed rails of increasing weights; others were primitive signals and early locking frames, showing the development of signal and point interlocking in the 1860s.

Amongst the small exhibits were notices, pictures, drawings, books and documents; railway company and Bradshaw's timetables; tickets made of metal, paper and card, dating from 1836 onwards; the first ticket-dating press, the invention of Thomas Edmondson on the Newcastle & Carlisle Railway in 1837; and a guard's timepiece kept in a locked case so that he could not tamper with it.

Here also was the Briggs collection, the third notable addition of 1927, given on condition that it would be displayed as a whole, which made the move to the new and more spacious accommodation essential. It had been collected by Isaac Briggs, the son of an early railway contractor, and consisted mainly of items from the period 1820–1850 relating to the early railway civil engineers, whose work, he felt, had not received sufficient attention. There were prints, engravings, lithographs, maps, books, and letters signed by the two Stephensons, Brunel, Timothy Hackworth, George Hudson and Edward Pease. Particularly delightful were a complete volume in splendid condition of *Bourne's drawings of the London and Birmingham Railway*, the series now well known, portraying construction of the line; and the volume of *Coloured views on the Liverpool and Manchester Railway, with plates of the coaches, machines, &c. From drawings made on the spot by Mr T.T. Bury*, beautiful coloured pictures published by the celebrated printmaker R. Ackermann in 1831. Before his death in 1926, Isaac Briggs had suggested to his daughter that the collection should be offered to the LNER, and she presented it in person on 31 May 1927.

The stations

When the first trains reached York in 1839, they had to use a temporary station while the medieval town wall was pierced by a wide archway and a terminus befitting the city's importance was built within. This was opened in January 1841 by the York & North Midland Railway, one of the constituents of the future North Eastern, whose tracks ran to Altofts Junction, near Normanton, on the Leeds–Derby line of the North Midland, whence there was rail communication with London Euston. Within a few

Early signals and locking frames
at Queen Street in 1927.

2-2-4 tank locomotive No 1679 attached to the Engineer's Inspection Saloon at York in the
summer of 1927. Built in 1860 as a 2-2-2, No 1679 was rebuilt in 1881. Her driving wheels
have inside bearings, whereas *Aerolite*'s were outside with brightly polished brass axle boxes.

years, trains reached York by other routes: from Darlington by the Great North of England Railway in March 1841; from Scarborough in 1845; from London King's Cross by the Great Northern in September 1850. All through trains between north and south had to reverse, locomotives were constantly moving in and out of the station, trains to and from Scarborough had to back between the terminus and the junction of the branch. Conflicting movements over the restricted approach led to confusion and delay. The only solution was to build a new station with through tracks and ample accommodation, but it was 1877 before the present station was opened.

The original train sheds of 1841 had no merit, but the exterior was a fine architectural composition designed by G. T. Andrews, an architect practising in York and a close personal friend of George Hudson, the 'Railway King', for whose railways Andrews provided many other excellent designs. His York station eventually had buildings on the eastern and western sides, and a hotel, completed in 1853, on the northern side between the platform ends and Rougier Street. All are still standing, and of the three it is the eastern arm, facing Tanner Row, that is the finest. Here was the main entrance, giving direct access to the departure platform through a colonnade of five columns carrying a corniced architrave. There are wings on either side, with arched windows on the ground floor, and two upper storeys stretching from end to end which have rectangular windows, all with stone dressings and generous cornices setting off the grey brick walls. After the later station had replaced it, the hotel and other buildings became railway offices, and a wall was built behind the colonnade. Even the warehouses Andrews

Railway Station, York.

The station of 1877, photographed before 1904. From an old postcard.

148

The York station of 1841, designed by G.T. Andrews, showing the colonnade which originally gave entrance to the departure platform. 26 August 1959.

The warehouses designed by G.T. Andrews for the first goods station at York. 26 August 1959.

designed for the goods station were – for these have been demolished – unusually distinguished.

The architect of the 1877 station was Thomas Prosser, but William Peachey was in charge when what was then the largest station in Britain was completed. Here, it is the interior that steals the show – 'train shed', although the correct term, seems inadequate. Few photographs do it justice, steam, smoke and long trains obscuring more or less of its splendours. In my collection, however, is a card postmarked 1913, but in fact issued about a decade earlier, as the footbridge erected in 1904 is absent. The anonymous photographer must have chosen his moment with the deliberate intention of getting an unobstructed view emphasing the structure, for there is nothing on the rails save a few far distant coaches! Even early in the century, such an occasion must have been very rare at York.

Six companies had running powers over North Eastern tracks into the station, so that during the short period when all were exercising them, locomotives in seven different liveries could be seen there, as well as at Carlisle. Great Northern engines brought main line trains from the south, as they had done into the old station since 1850. Midland trains came from Rotherham and beyond when the direct route via the Swinton & Knottingley Joint Line, avoiding Normanton, was opened in 1879. The Lancashire & Yorkshire began to run in from Altofts Junction, Normanton, in 1884. Great Eastern trains, even from Liverpool Street, came, like the Great Northern ones, via Doncaster and Shaftholme Junction, after 1892. From 1893 to

York–Leeds train leaving York, Sunday, 3 July 1927, behind North Eastern 4-4-0 No 1877. Touring theatrical companies travelled by the Sunday trains, taking their scenery in special Scenery Vans, one of which is the third vehicle in this train; perhaps more was in the container loaded on the fourth. The actors themselves were no doubt in the second, an ECJS vehicle which may have come from Newcastle.

150

Exhibition in York station on Sunday 17 June 1928. On the left, between platforms 10 and 11: NE 3-cylinder mixed traffic 4-6-0 No 911, class S3, built at Darlington 1923; Gresley 3-cylinder 2-6-0 No 39, built at Darlington 1924: Sentinel 100hp steam shunting locomotive No 81, built 1927; breakdown crane. In the centre, alongside platform 11: Sentinel-Cammell railcar *Teazle*. On the right, alongside platform 12: first class restaurant car No 22128, built at York in 1925 to NER design with British standard type concertina gangways; first class Pullman Car *Irene*; M&NEJPS mail van with pick-up net, built at York in 1904 to Midland design for the Newcastle–Bristol service.

Steam breakdown crane built by Cowans & Sheldon, Carlisle, in 1916, capable of lifting 35 tons at a radius of 23 feet; and Sentinel-Cammell steam railcar *Teazle*, built 1928 and painted cream and green. Seating 59 passengers. Designed for a speed of 36 mph. Boiler pressure 275 lb per square inch.

151

1904, the London & North Western exercised the right to run its own trains from Leeds to York. The Great Central began services from Sheffield and beyond via Swinton & Knottingley in 1899.

Locomotives and rolling stock of great variety were still to be seen in and around the station in 1927, for although Great Eastern engines no longer came after 1922, its coaches did, on the Continental Express with destination boards reading 'Harwich Parkeston Quay – Ipswich – Spalding – Sleaford – Lincoln – Doncaster – York', rivalling the lengthy roof boards favoured by the Great Western. East Coast expresses, made up with some of the finest vehicles in Britain, were brought in by Great Northern Atlantics or, more frequently, Gresley Pacifics. The familiar Midland class 2 4-4-0s collected through coaches for Bristol, brought in by the North Eastern from Newcastle, and attached them to other clerestory coaches, which at some point would acquire a restaurant car. Lancashire & Yorkshire Atlantics, Hughes four-cylinder 4-6-0s, and new LMS 2-6-0s designed by Hughes, headed trains of L&Y coaches starting from a bay platform, or took over from the North Eastern the Newcastle–Liverpool restaurant car express.

The Great Central on its own provided a feast for train-spotters, for although its passenger engines were all 4-4-0s of J.G. Robinson's 1901 design, they brought not only local trains of their own, but also the through restaurant car sets running via Banbury on the cross-country services developed by Sam Fay. The splendid stock built specially by the GC in 1911 for the Newcastle–Bournemouth run alternated with an inferior London & South Western set, until replaced in 1929 by comfortable new Southern Railway coaches of Maunsell's design with Buckeye couplings and Pullman type gangways. Another similar GC train alternated with elderly Great Western Dean clerestory coaches between Newcastle and Swansea. There was also the Newcastle-Southampton train, less distinguished, alternately GW and GC stock, which had picked up a through coach from Glasgow; and the 6.25 p.m. York to Swindon which took on the Aberdeen–Penzance coach, alternately a North British or Great Western vehicle, attached at York to Gresley's triplet set, or to GW vehicles, each including a restaurant car. The various York locomotive sheds therefore housed a number of 'foreign' engines in addition to a galaxy of North Eastern and LNER ones. Even so, the supply of 'home' locomotives could be overtaxed on a summer Saturday, when incoming 'foreign' excursion trains needed to change engines, so that it was not uncommon for Midland, L&Y, GN and GC locomotives to take their trains on to Scarborough, the driver accompanied on the footplate by a North Eastern pilotman.

East Coast Train Runner

In 1929, postings followed one another with bewildering rapidity. Back to beloved York in May, a very short spell in the timetable section of the

Superintendent's department was succeeded in June by one in the District Goods Manager's office in Leeds. I dislike commuting, but as the train service between the two towns was good and I had found excellent, though simple, lodgings in the pleasant garden suburb of New Earswick, I stayed on there. It was as well, because about the middle of July I was back with the timetable section as 'East Coast Train Runner'. This involved much travelling, principally betwen York and Edinburgh, checking the timekeeping, suggesting ways of improving punctuality. It was an experience I thoroughly enjoyed. A train I was enjoined to watch closely was the 7.45 p.m. from Waverley, a notoriously poor timekeeper. It was a very second rate East Coast express, rolling into York about 3 a.m., but amongst its assorted vehicles for King's Cross was a sleeping car. This was certainly very convenient for Northumbrians, as the train called at most of the main line stations in the county (a berth was sometimes occupied by Viscount Grey of Fallodon, one time Foreign Secretary, who boarded the train at his private station). But it had a tail of fish vans, from Mallaig, Peterhead and Aberdeen for Newcastle, York, Doncaster and King's Cross, and these were its bugbear.

Owing to late arrival of connecting trains at Waverley, the fish vans could not always be marshalled in the correct order for detaching. Furthermore, among the boxes of fish for the van's destination there were some for other stations en route. I remember one early morning at York when the station pilot engine was remarshalling the tail and porters were running alongside the moving vans lifting boxes of fish from van to platform! Loss of time at stations was inevitable, and the only cure was for more selective loading at the ports; but neither the North British over the steeply graded West Highland line, nor the Great North of Scotland over the long branch from Peterhead, was inclined to haul, say, two half-filled vans when one would suffice.

I was not expected in the office except when I had a report to make out, so my day began with departure from York on the Flying Scotsman about 2 p.m., and I dined on Waverley station before my return, en route drinking tea with the friendly sleeping-car attendant. If I had not been on that turn the previous night, I would catch the morning train from York, the prestigious 8.55 a.m. Leeds to Glasgow, at that date generally hauled by one of Gresley's handsome new Shire class three-cylinder 4-4-0s. This enabled me to spend about five hours exploring Edinburgh: the castle, Holyrood Palace, Craigmillar Castle on the outskirts. But, as it was not always necessary to ride that wayward 7.45 from Edinburgh itself, sometimes as I went north I changed into a stopping train at Newcastle, and visited Berwick or the Northumbrian castles at Norham, Warkworth, and the little known but very interesting one at Edlingham, dining at a local hotel before catching the train at the nearest main line station.

Another of the East Coast Train Runner's duties involved Saturday

The first of the Shire class, No 234 *Yorkshire*, built at Darlington in 1927. A 4-4-0 for secondary main line duties, it was designed by Gresley, who had been impressed by the performance of Robinson's Improved Director class in Scotland. Driving wheels 6ft 8in in diameter, 3 cylinders 17in by 26in, boiler pressure 180lb per square inch. From a contemporary postcard.

afternoons and long evenings on York station, and there was enough of the enthusiast in me then (as now) to find pleasure in that. The passage of the far north sleeping car trains between 11 p.m. and midnight demanded attention. These could often be delayed while Post Office servants loaded and unloaded mail bags. The most interesting night was that preceding the opening of the grouse shooting season, a night on which the sleeping-car trains ran in several portions, each with locomotive and dining car to be detached at York. There would also be trains of motor car vans, and occasionally a privately hired special. Both up and down main platforms would be used by these, but even so, the headlamps of the next train would be seen as it stood beside the great Locomotive Yard signal cabin, waiting until a platform was free; amongst them would be the Great Central train from Banbury conveying the Penzance–Aberdeen coach, whose passengers would be lucky if there was time for it to make the connection with the Aberdeen express from King's Cross and for them to avail themselves of the advertised facility of sleeping berths. Drivers of the fresh locomotives backed on carefully to avoid disturbing sleeping passengers (for the time was approaching midnight), though seldom as softly as one I witnessed, who controlled his 92 tons of steel with such expertise that the buffers just kissed.

Free time in mornings and at weekends during that summer of 1929 were spent exploring the city of York, not the locomotive sheds! Wearing still the air of a provincial capital, York has so much to offer a student of medieval, Tudor, and seventeenth- and eighteenth-century architecture. It is a city I love, and repeated visits not only stimulate interest, but confer on me an extraordinary peace of mind.

154

Lancashire & Yorkshire train leaving York station in the summer of 1927 behind Hughes 4-cylinder 4-6-0 No 10439, built in 1923. The class was a greatly improved version from 1920 onwards of that introduced by George Hughes in 1908.

No 2558 *Tracery* threading the up mid-day Scotsman through the crossover from the platform to the main line on 11 May 1927.

Newcastle–Southampton train, the GWR set strengthened with two NE non-corridor clerestory coaches in front, and the through coach from Glasgow probably in rear. Great Central 4-4-0 No 6030 piloting North Eastern class S2 4-6-0 No 813. At Chaloners Whin, 3 September 1927. Chaloners Whin (there have been several variants of the spelling) was where the NE main line through Selby to the end-on junction with the Great Northern at Askern, near Doncaster, diverged from that to Church Fenton. At the latter junction, the Leeds line was joined by that through Burton Salmon and over the Swinton & Knottingley Joint Line to the Midland's and Great Central's routes to Sheffield. Trains seen here therefore provided plenty of variety.

York–Harwich Continental express with through coach from Glasgow. This would not normally have been a turn for the Great Central engine, but it was a Saturday afternoon (3 September 1927) when locomotives were apt to be in short supply, and No 5113 had probably been called upon to take the train to Doncaster, where a Great Eastern engine would take over.

Scarborough–Leeds express. North Eastern class S 4-6-0 No 753 had previously been photographed on a freight train at Hett, County Durham. 3 September 1927.

The Scarborough Flier gathering way on its non-stop run to King's Cross behind No 2543 *Melton*, Saturday, 3 September 1927. The Flier was a train first introduced under LNER management.

No 2576 *The White Knight* taking the down mid-day Scotsman round the curve from the north end of the station. 7 May 1927.

A determined effort to beat the Great Western's twenty-three year old record of the longest non-stop run, Paddington to Plymouth, 225.7 miles; *Flying Fox* passing York on 11 July 1927, with the first non-stop run from King's Cross to Newcastle, 268.3 miles.

North Eastern 4-4-2 No 1680, class V, at the coaling stage north of York station. Designed by Wilson Worsdell, the ten class V were the first NE Atlantics, 1903. Driving wheels 6ft 10in in diameter, 2 cylinders 20in by 28in, boiler pressure 200lb per square inch. April 1927.

North Eastern 4-4-0 No 1239 class R1 at York, 10 May 1927. This very handsome class, one of the finest looking on any British railway, was designed by Wilson Worsdell and introduced in 1908. Ten were built for express passenger work with the high, for that date, boiler pressure of 225lb per square inch. Cylinders were 19in by 26in. The total weight was 59½ tons, 42 tons of which were carried on the 6ft 10in driving wheels. She was standing at the back of the big Locomotive Yard signal cabin controlling the entry to the station from the south.

North Eastern 4-4-2 No 2163, class Z. She had been fitted experimentally by Gresley with a Dabeg feed-water heater, but the economy in coal and water consumption was insufficient to justify the expense of fitting the equipment. 7 May 1927.

North Eastern 4-6-2 No 2403 *City of Durham* alongside York station in the summer of 1927. The Cities were impressive to look at, handsome as all North Eastern passenger locomotives were, but it has been said that they were not noticeably better than the class Z Atlantics.

This Hull & Barnsley 0-6-0 would never have got anywhere near York before 1922! Built by Kitson & Co. in 1889 to the designs of Matthew Stirling, H&B Locomotive Superintendent 1885-1922, No 53 had been renumbered 2433 and slightly modified by the NER, for she originally had a domeless boiler in the Stirling tradition of Matthew's father, Patrick, and uncle, James, of the GNR and South Eastern respectively. At York South Shed, May 1927.

Great Northern 2-cylinder 2-6-0 No 4673 outside the shed at the south end of the station used by GN locomotives. 11 May 1927.

Great Central No 5213, built in 1909, outside the south shed on 7 May 1927. Not even J.G. Robinson could make an 0-8-0 look graceful. The fore-and-aft overhang was even more pronounced in the NE classes. Introduced in 1903, these GC engines had 4ft 7in wheels, 2 cylinders 19 inches by 26 inches, and a working pressure of 180lb per square inch.

Lancashire & Yorkshire 4-4-2 No 10335, when the day's work was over, at the shed used by LMS engines, which was formerly the boiler shop of the repair works set up by the York & North Midland Railway in 1842. She was one of the Atlantics introduced in 1899 by J.A.F. Aspinall, Chief Mechanical Engineer 1886–99. 23 July 1927.

LMS 2-6-0 No 13002 outside the shed, 16 July 1927. The class was designed by George Hughes, Chief Mechanical Engineer of the L&Y since 1904, and of the LMS 1923–25. The first of this class appeared in 1926, and a total of 245 was built, working very successfully all over the LMS system, even on the Highland. The cylinders were steeply inclined to meet the restrictions imposed by the civil engineer in order to clear platform and the lower parts of other lineside structures.

CHAPTER TEN

ENVOI

Between my postings to York in 1927–28 and again in 1929, I was sent to the goods stations in Ripon and Harrogate. The handling and recording of goods followed what seemed an archaic and unnecessarily complex system, common to all the railways in Britain. Long invoices were made out in triplicate; one copy was kept, one was sent to the destination station, and the third accompanied the consignment. On them was recorded the name and address of the consignee, the nature of the goods, weight, charge calculated according to mileage and an elaborate classification, whether carriage was paid by sender or was to be collected from the consignee, and the route to be followed, naming the junction points with other railways, even those which had become part of the LNER in 1923. The man-hours spent filling in, checking and sorting the invoices was prodigious. While some such documentation was probably necessary for traffic moving in wagon loads, individual 'small parcels' (not necessarily small, in fact anything less than a wagon load) might surely have been dealt with in a more simple way. 'Small parcels' spent a shocking time in transit, sent from one tranship point to another, handled many times with all the attendant risk of damage, pilfering and sometimes loss.

I enjoyed lodging in Ripon, a small city of great charm, with a spacious market place, and a Minster, cathedral only since 1836, which is an intriguing mixture of styles from Wilfrid's seventh-century Saxon crypt to sixteenth-century rebuilding left unfinished at the Reformation. Set amid picturesque pastoral and arable land, and linked to the River Ure by a short canal, the town proved a very pleasant centre for evening walks beside river or canal or along country lanes, and for weekend bicycle rides.

The passenger station, on the line originally built by the Leeds Northern Railway from Leeds through Harrogate and Northallerton to Stockton, had unusual dignity, and a waiting room with stained glass windows, befitting the royal and other distinguished visitors to the Marquis of Ripon at Studley

165

Royal. There was no longer a marquis in 1928, but nevertheless the Duke and Duchess of York stepped off the Pullman one day, the Duchess smiling on us with that charm which has since endeared her to the nation as Queen and Queen Mother.

The stationmaster was an efficient, pleasant man, but under him the goods station was managed by a chief clerk, a crabbed little man, probably a disappointed one. It was the only office in which I met resentment at my position as a trainee, most marked after I had been twice recalled temporarily to York. The chief clerk had a favourite, a conceited young man who, in the opinion of his senior, was far more worthy and capable than myself: insofar as goods station accounting was concerned, I will concede that he was justified!

At the much larger goods station in Harrogate, the atmosphere was friendly, even 'matey'. But in spite of its trees and open spaces, Harrogate is not a type of town I care for. Nevertheless, it was a gateway to lovely country, in particular the beautiful and secluded Nidderdale.

In October 1929 I was moved to Sunderland, so I hoped to rejoin the community at Hylton, but when I talked to Matt Wilson in the cabin and my former landlady in Primrose street, I found a village still reeling from its shock of fifteen months before. There was no alternative but to search for lodgings in Sunderland.

There is really little more to say. I had made the grade – I had been a Traffic Apprentice since early in the summer – but at considerable cost in personal stress and strain. The frequent transfers were unsettling, and although many kind friends had provided me with introductions, contacts made were soon severed by new postings. So it became a solitary life, with little relaxation from work and study. Moreover, there grew a desire for a career divorced from any form of commerce, one that entailed some form of direct service to others. I decided to teach; perhaps it was predictable from educational influences at home, and the interest I had felt in the young railwaymen I had met. I resigned from the LNER at the end of January 1930. There have been moments of disillusion, of course, but I have never seriously regretted making the change. A lifetime spent teaching young boys has been a happy, and, I hope, a useful one. Nevertheless, I have always been grateful for experience gained outside the four walls of a classroom, and, as any reader of this book will realise, I have never lost my interest in railways.

At York there was genuine regret at my leaving; and while I was preparing this book, especially the early pages of Chapter Three, the feeling came upon me that perhaps I had betrayed a trust, for the LNER had treated me well. This was dispelled when I re-read two treasured letters. My mother – for it was she who, against all the odds, had established the personal contact in 1925 – had written to King's Cross when I handed in my resignation. She had received a reply, of course. Surprisingly, I too received a personal letter, also hand-written (and Sir Ralph Wedgwood wrote a beautifully formed script). In it, there was no suggestion that I had failed; instead, he remarked upon things I had done well, and wished me success in the future. As I have written previously, he was one who showed sympathetic understanding and great courtesy, traits not always evident in a great administrator.

BIBLIOGRAPHY

AND

THE INITIAL QUESTION

BIBLIOGRAPHY

Ahrons, E.L.: *The British Steam Railway Locomotive 1825–1925*; London, Locomotive Publishing Co. 1927, reprinted Ian Allan 1966.

Allen, Cecil J.: *The Great Eastern Railway*: 5th edition; London, Ian Allan 1968. *The North Eastern Railway*; 2nd edition; London, Ian Allan 1974. *The London & North Eastern Railway*; London, Ian Allan 1966.

Basset-Lowke Railways; A Commemorative Edition 1969.

Biddle, Gordon, and Nock, O.S.: *The Railway Heritage of Britain*; London, Michael Joseph 1983.

Bonavia, Michael R.: *The Four Great Railways*; Newton Abbot, David & Charles 1980. *A History of the LNER. The First Years, 1923–33*; London, George Allen & Unwin 1982.

Bulleid, H.A.V.: *Master Builders of Steam*; London, Ian Allan 1963.

Cox, E.S.: *Locomotive Panorama* Vol. 1; London, Ian Allan 1965.

Hennessey, R.A.S.: *The Electric Railway that Never Was, York–Newcastle 1919*; Newcastle, Oriel Press 1970.

Holcroft, H.: *Locomotive Adventure, Fifty Years with Steam*; London, Ian Allan *c*.1965.

Holt, Tonie and Valmai: *Picture Postcards of the Golden Age*; London, MacGibbon & Kee 1971.

Hoole, K.: *The Railways of York*; Dalesman Books 1976. *The East Coast Main Line since 1925*; London, Ian Allan 1977. *North Eastern Branch Lines since 1925*; London, Ian Allan 1978. *North Eastern Branch Lines Past and Present*; Poole, Oxford Publishing Co. 1984.

Jenkin-Jones, C.M.: *The North Eastern Railway, A Centenary Story*; York, British Railways (North Eastern Region) 1954.

London & North Eastern Railway Magazine 1927.

Marshall, John: *A Biographical Dictionary of Railway Engineers*; Newton Abbot, David & Charles 1978.

Nock, O.S.: *The British Steam Railway Locomotive 1925–65*; London, Ian Allan 1966. *Steam Railways in Retrospect*; London, A. & C. Black 1966. *The Pocket Encyclopaedia of British Steam Locomotives in Colour*; London, Blandford

Press 1964. *Steam Railways of Britain in Colour*; London, Blandford Press 1967.

Parkes, G.D.: *The Hull & Barnsley Railway*; The Oakwood Press 1959.

Railway Year Book, various issues for the early 1920s.

Reder, Gustav, translated by C. Hamilton Ellis: *Clockwork, Steam and Electric, A History of Model Railways*; London, Ian Allan 1972.

Robbins, Michael: *The Railway Age*; London, Routledge & Kegan Paul 1962.

Sinclair, Neil: *The River Wear. A Pictorial Survey from Biddick to the River Mouth*; Tyne and Wear County Council Museums 1984.

Staff, Frank: *The Picture Postcard and its Origins*; London, Lutterworth Press 1979.

Thomas, John: *The West Highland Railway*; Newton Abbot, David & Charles 1965.

THE INITIAL QUESTION

CLC, Cheshire Lines Committee, jointly owned by the Great Central, Great Northern and Midland Railway Companies.

ECJS, East Coast Joint Stock, the passenger rolling stock provided for Anglo-Scottish services by the Great Northern, North British and North Eastern Companies.

GCR, Great Central Railway.

GER, Great Eastern Railway.

GNR, Great Northern Railway.

GWR, Great Western Railway.

LHJC, Lambton Hetton & Joicey Collieries, a combine of colliery owners in County Durham.

L&YR, Lancashire & Yorkshire Railway.

LBSCR, London Brighton & South Coast Railway.

LMS, London Midland & Scottish Railway, one of the groups formed in 1923.

LNER, London & North Eastern Railway, one of the groups formed in 1923.

LNWR, London & North Western Railway.

LSWR, London & South Western Railway.

M&NB, Midland and North British joint ownership of Anglo-Scottish passenger rolling stock.

M&NEJPS, Midland & North Eastern Joint Postal Stock used on the Newcastle–Bristol mail trains.

MSJ&A, Manchester South Junction & Altrincham Railway, jointly owned by the Great Central and London & North Western Railway Companies.

NER, North Eastern Railway.

SE&CR, South Eastern & Chatham Railway Companies' Joint Managing Committee.

SR, Southern Railway, one of the groups formed in 1923.

INDEX

INDEX